ADVANCE PRAISE

"Michael's authenticity in opening up about his struggle through addiction, as well as his experiences in entrepreneurship and challenges he overcame, give a keen insight into the mindset shifts throughout his journey. Chasing the High is an inspirational read that I highly recommend for anyone dealing with the highs and lows of life."

—LEWIS HOWES, NY TIMES BESTSELLING AUTHOR, THE SCHOOL OF GREATNESS; AUTHOR, THE MASK OF MASCULINITY; HOST OF TOP 50 RANKED PODCAST ON ITUNES, THE SCHOOL OF GREATNESS; LIFESTYLE ENTREPRENEUR, BUSINESS COACH, KEYNOTE SPEAKER

"Chasing the High reveals the addictive struggles many people face but often mask. Traveling from the depths of misery, it's a journey to the ultimate happiness: self-love."

—JAMES WHITTAKER, BESTSELLING AUTHOR, *THINK AND GROW RICH: THE LEGACY*

"*Chasing the High is for anyone who needs to shift from addictive patterns and negative beliefs to positive and lasting habits. Michael takes us on a journey through gambling, money, meditation, and growth. He teaches us what true success looks like, and more importantly, what that success feels like.*"

—JULES SCHROEDER, FOUNDER, UNCONVENTIONAL LIFE, A GLOBAL COMMUNITY OF ENTREPRENEURS, CREATIVES, AND THOUGHT LEADERS; HOST OF TOP-RANKED PODCAST UNCONVENTIONAL LIFE SHOW; INC. MAGAZINE'S #1 OF THE TOP 27 FEMALE ENTREPRENEURS CHANGING THE WORLD IN 2017

"*Michael's journey through addiction, entrepreneurship, and the battles he overcame throughout shows the raw emotions and struggles many go through. His ability to come out on the other side a better person are inspiring and motivating. Chasing the High is a must read.*"

—VIRGINIA SALAS KASTILIO, FOUNDER, *GINI.TV* AND *I TRUST YOU*; *INC.* MAGAZINE'S #6 OF THE TOP 27 FEMALE ENTREPRENEURS CHANGING THE WORLD IN 2017

"*All entrepreneurs are addicts in one form or another, whether we admit it or not. Chasing the High is a must-read for all entrepreneurs. It will help you overcome your own obstacles in business and in life. This book made me feel like I'm not alone and has helped me cope with my own highs.*"

—BRANDON T. ADAMS, EMMY® AWARD-WINNING PRODUCER AND TV SERIES HOST, *SUCCESS IN YOUR CITY*

CHASING THE HIGH

CHASING

THE

HIGH

AN ENTREPRENEUR'S MINDSET
THROUGH ADDICTION, LAWSUITS,
AND HIS JOURNEY TO THE EDGE

MICHAEL G. DASH

LIONCREST
PUBLISHING

CHASING THE HIGH
An Entrepreneur's Mindset Through Addiction,
Lawsuits, and His Journey to the Edge

ISBN   978-1-5445-0349-3 *Hardcover*
       978-1-5445-0347-9 *Paperback*
       978-1-5445-0348-6 *Ebook*

I'd like to dedicate this book to everyone who has contributed to my journey, both past and present. I could not have made this transformation without the tools and enlightenment you have all provided. Special thanks to Jules Schroeder, Justin Faerman and Jackie Knetchel, my brothers and sisters in YEC and Activation, Michael Fazio, the Gamblers Anonymous program, Jay Dash, Libby Payne, my former employees at Parallel HR Solutions, Inc., and my parents, Lynn and Bernie Dash. Thank you all for your unwavering love, support, and friendship.

To anyone dealing with addiction or isolation challenges, recovery is one act away. Take that first step.

CONTENTS

INTRODUCTION

A GAMBLING LIFE

I discovered gambling over dessert one Thanksgiving. I was eleven.

I remember the moment distinctly. My family had made the annual trip from New Jersey to Massachusetts to celebrate the holiday. My brother and I sat next to my uncle on my grandmother's couch watching college football—a tradition, and something that fed our passion for sports.

"Why are you rooting so hard for Notre Dame?" I asked my uncle. "Do you really like them or something?"

"I have one hundred dollars on them," he said, pulling a gambling card from his pocket and explaining that he had multiple bets going on at once. "If they win—along with these three other teams—I win ten to one *plus* the profits from my original bet."

My brother and I were mesmerized. Watching sports and winning money—what could be better?

"Here," my uncle said. "I can give you one of these cards if you want to bet on tomorrow's NFL games. If you give me ten dollars and you get all four games right, you'll win one hundred dollars."

Oh my God, I thought. *I have to do this.* One hundred dollars sounded like a fortune!

My brother, who was almost eight at the time, followed me over to where my father was in the kitchen. He was talking about his business with some of the other adults. I knew my father was more likely to give me money than my mother, who would have certainly questioned it.

"Dad, can I have ten dollars? We're going to the store to get hoagies." As soon as he handed over the money, my brother and I started deliberating on what teams we should circle for the next day. After about two hours, we made our selections and brought the card—and our bet—to my uncle.

We were glued to the television more than usual the following afternoon as we watched the football game and tracked our bets. We won the first three games, and the final one was in the evening. We defended the television in the living room fiercely. Anytime someone came in and wanted to change the channel, we wouldn't let them. How could we? We were *this close* to winning one hundred dollars.

And we did. All four of our teams won that day, and we couldn't have been more excited. Our uncle paid us. It was more money than I'd ever had at one time. There was something else, though, that excited me—something *besides* the hundred dollars burning a hole in my pocket. It was the adrenaline. The rush. The risk. And winning was an added benefit.

I gambled for the next twenty years straight.

THE EVOLUTION OF AN ADDICT

My father was an entrepreneur and owned an import-export business and a retail store in New Jersey, and when I was growing up, I worked for him regularly. So did my Little League baseball coach, who came in for shifts on weekends. The guys at the store talked gambling nonstop, and I was a good listener. I knew they usually went to the Meadowlands Racetrack after work to bet on horses.

"Hey," I said to my coach one day. "I want to come with you to the track. Tell my dad you're taking me home, and you can sneak me in."

The racetrack was about half an hour from work—a straight shot down Route 17, except for a handful of toll-booths along the way. Back then, each toll was forty-five cents, and my coach taught me an ingenious way to find some more money on the trip to the track. At every toll-booth, my coach would open his door and grab all the change on the ground left behind by drivers who had missed the collection bucket.

"I just got two dollars! That's two dollars more I can play on the horses!" he'd say. I did that same thing for the next fifteen years, scooping change off the ground just as he had. It was exhilarating in a strange way—like I'd won something. Back then, though, I just thought he was a little weird and crazy.

Once I got inside the racetrack, I'd ask my coach what horses he liked. I also looked for any interesting horse names that jumped out at me. As I glanced through all the names, there it was: "Magical Mike." How could I not bet on a horse that had the same name as me? I mean, what better reason could there be? So, I gave my coach my money and had him place the bet. We'd sit in the stands together and watch with that feeling of exhilaration as the horses rounded the track. I did that for years. Nobody bothered us.

When we couldn't make it to the track, the coach and I and some other friends would go to offtrack betting (OTB) in a neighboring town. There, in that dingy, depressing room with smoke hovering over us from all the cigarettes, the races were simulcast. We—along with mostly men in their fifties, sixties, and seventies—would spend entire days at OTB. It was always the same: find cool horses' names or some other mostly illogical reason, bet, watch, repeat.

I continued to gamble as I got older, and I started dabbling in card games when I was twelve. My friends and I, including my brother, would play what we called acey-deucy—or high-low—trying to win whatever pot we could throw together. Two cards were dealt, and whoever's turn it was would bet—as much as the size of the pot—if the third card would land between the first two. The pots were small at first, but they grew very quickly.

At sixteen, I got a job at a Travel Mart at a rest stop along the Garden State Parkway. Wearing my visor and name tag, I'd sell donuts, coffee, and newspapers to travelers and collect my weekly paycheck—a paycheck that I would promptly gamble at the weekly card game. All of it. And because I was one of the only ones in my group of friends old enough to have a job, I also had a bank account and a checkbook. I thought to myself, *I am going to bring my checkbook to the card games and write checks to put in the pot.* That felt so powerful. In a small high school with only eighty-nine students in my graduating class, everybody in my circle knew me as the guy with the checkbook. Throughout high school, I gambled on sports, horses, and cards. Still, I was an above-average student, an athlete, and president of the student council, but gambling was more important than all.

When it came time to choose a college, I wanted to attend a school that was far enough away from my parents so they couldn't drop in unannounced yet still close enough so I could drive home when I wanted. After visiting several universities, I stepped foot onto the campus of the University of Maryland and immediately fell in love. It was the opposite of the small high school I was trying to escape, and I was in awe. I enrolled immediately and found a door-to-door sales job selling vinyl windows, roofing, siding, and decks to some of the most diverse, poverty-stricken areas in Washington, DC, and Maryland. I had a strong personality and was an excellent salesperson. I was driven and worked hard. Despite enduring dogs running through screens and biting me (true story) and having homeowners believe I was trying to swindle them into home improvements they didn't need, I was successful and made good money. Going door to door is a true test of one's ability to adapt to any situation thrown at them and really drives you to think on your feet! I didn't know at the time, but it prepared me for so many other jobs I had in my life. Making good money here allowed me to continue my gambling ways.

My gambling escalated. My college roommate introduced me to his bookie from New Jersey. At the time, I didn't understand most bookies were associated with the mafia and were not to be messed with. I was just a college kid with money to bet. I was naive and didn't have a care in the world.

I gambled through entire paychecks and entire weekends with my roommate and any other gamblers who wanted to join. I experimented with different drugs, partied, and only attended class when it was convenient for me. Instead of going to most lectures, I'd skip them and buy TerpNotes—a nod to the Maryland Terrapins—from students who actually went to class and took scrupulous notes. They then sold those notes at the student union. I was one of their biggest customers. Then, when it was time for an exam, I'd pop as many Ritalin as needed and would stay up for days studying my precious TerpNotes.

As I partied more, I saw an opportunity to make more money to feed my gambling and party habits. So I started dealing drugs. I hadn't even touched a drug until smoking marijuana my senior year of high school, and only a few years later, I was dealing them. It took my entrepreneurial desires to another level. One year, I asked my father to borrow his Lincoln Continental, and on spring break, I drove it from the University of Maryland to the University of New Mexico, where one of my friends was attending school. Back then, a pound of marijuana could be sold for about $1,000 in Maryland, and it could be purchased for approximately $300 in New Mexico. I saw an opportunity and took advantage.

On that trip I transported more than twenty pounds and delivered it to the purchaser. I made approximately $14,000. It was money I had never dreamed of at the time, and the temptation of it drove me to these actions. I was reckless and never thought of consequences, completely living in another reality at the time. I had "big man on campus" syndrome.

After that trip, I subsequently went to Atlantic City with a few of my college friends and spent three days in a drug-induced gambling stupor, spending and gambling all of that money away—yes, all of it. It was sick behavior, but I chalked it up to an amazing adventure at the time and thought college life was going smoothly. That was, until my roommate was shot in the arm with a .357 Magnum. The shooter was his ex-girlfriend—who happened to be our bookie's daughter. After the incident, I began using different bookies, shopping around to see who would give me the best spread for the games. As I started to lose on a lot of the games I was betting, I observed that a lot of my gambling friends were also losing. I thought to myself, *Why be a gambler if I can be a bookie?* When my roommate returned the following semester, we decided to go into the bookie business. We were making bets with other bookies and taking bets from other students. It was the biggest rush I ever felt.

My roommate had just returned from being shot in the arm, so he was doing physical therapy to regain the strength and feeling he had lost. One day, he invited me to come over to the new place where he was living. In his room and on top of his drawer were bottles of pills...*lots* of bottles of *lots* of pills. He started explaining to me what all these pills were and why he needed them. I was intrigued and curious and also looking for the next high. He told me what I should try, and I listened. Experimenting with pills led me to experimenting with other drugs. I never thought of the consequences. I was living in another world and experimented as much as I could, which led to taking steroids. This new routine now included working out at the gym excessively, using drugs, and gambling. This drove how hard I worked in the door-to-door home improvement business. I held it together on the outside, but on the inside, I lived in a manic state, one of the many times in my life I lived this way. I continually was chasing the high—any high and multiple highs at the same time.

One was never good enough, but a combination of highs made me feel *alive*, and I always wanted more.

PROFESSIONAL SUCCESS, PERSONAL TURMOIL

When I graduated from college, I felt like I was in a good spot. I could gamble and party yet still take care of my responsibilities. My grades showed I was a decent student because I would do what I needed to be above average, and I'd always been exceptional at selling whatever it was that I was selling. Because I was obsessed with sports and excellent at sales, I landed a position in sports advertising for a company called University Sports Publications. My job was to sell advertising in more than five hundred college sports publications across the country. I was responsible for calling businesses that were working at these various universities and encouraging them to purchase ad space in a college football or basketball program that was sold at the games on campus. I knew the sales pitch, and I *killed it* with clients, becoming a manager in only two years.

While there, I became close with the owner, who, of course, was a gambler himself. We discussed sports betting and played poker games after work consistently. He regularly encouraged the gambling, and I consistently followed his lead. He was my boss, and I looked up to him at the time.

After four years of success professionally but chaos personally, I realized that I really wasn't aligned with his business practices and the way he manipulated his employees and me. After I had grown close with him, he called me into his office one day. He asked me what my opinion was of several of the employees both senior and junior to me. As a naive employee a few years out of college, I was honest to a fault and told him exactly what I thought. I felt like we were tight and he was asking me because he respected and trusted my opinion. Boy, was I wrong. The following day, I watched him march every employee he had asked me about into his office one by one, walking right past my desk where I sat. As I watched this, my heart dropped to the floor and there was a pit in my stomach. *What was I witnessing? Was he really telling them what I shared with him? Why would he do this?* Every person left his office and stared me down with a look of anger and disgust on their face. They were *not* happy with me, and I felt duped by the owner. Not understanding why he did what he did, I had to rebuild my relationships with my coworkers, but it was never the same, and I had made my mind up that I was going to leave if something like this ever happened again. And of course, it did, but to another one of my coworkers. I spoke up and said something to the owner after witnessing this. I told him what I really thought of this behavior, had a disagreement with him, and resigned that day. I had no backup plan, no job. I just knew that I could no longer work for someone with these types of morals, no matter how much money I was making, and I was doing very well at the time.

Soon after, I was having lunch in New York City with my best friend I grew up with when he presented an idea.

"Why don't you come work with me at the professional staffing company I am running?" he asked. It was a generous offer. He had just been promoted to president, and I figured if I could sell home improvements door to door and sell ad space over the phone, I could surely sell talent.

I was intrigued by his idea and decided to take him up on it—only, I wanted to work for another staffing company first and learn on their dime instead of his. I did not want to be a burden and knew he didn't have time to teach me the ropes, so I went to work for a technology staffing business: Hall Kinion, a company that was eventually bought out by Kforce, one of the top five search firms in the US. It was 1998, and my first task was to sell computer development and IT staffing services and personnel. There was only one problem: I was so computer illiterate that the first day I came in the office and tried to turn my computer on, I was hitting the disc eject button over and over thinking it was the power button! See, I hadn't used a computer at my previous job and barely used it in college. The computer wasn't turning on, and I turned to my manager and asked him why they would set me up with a broken computer on my first day. He looked at me and watched as I continued to think the disk eject button was the power button. He later explained to me that he thought hiring me was a huge mistake. After having to be shown how to turn a computer on, I knew I needed to partner up with someone who was tech savvy to show me the ropes. With the help of a colleague who mentored me, I soon got the hang of it.

The business was split between sales and recruiting. While I was focusing on selling technology staffing services, we had teams of recruiters who were focused on finding the talent to fulfill the job orders the sales team was bringing in. I was having success bringing in business from companies like Sony and Bear Stearns, and I started closing many deals with one of the senior recruiters who had a solid understanding of technology. We formed a good team. I was strong on the client and sales side, and she was strong on the technical recruiting and screening side. However, the terror attack on 9/11 changed everything. Soon thereafter, she moved back to her home state of Utah, and I—feeling ready—took the position working as the director of business development for my friend's staffing company. I transitioned from selling technology staffing to selling administrative staffing services—a high-volume, low-margin business, and one I learned quickly. In just four years, I grew my book of business to over $4 million in revenue, and as a company, we grew to the $11 million mark.

My years in New York City were outwardly successful and inwardly destructive. Because I was making more money, I had more money to gamble with—and I did even though I rarely won. The rush and the high of gambling was much more important than if I won or lost. Placing the bet itself was where I experienced the high that was controlling my life. As I continued to gamble uncontrollably, I spiraled into debt. Living in New York City fed my out-of-control personality, and I continued experimenting with drugs, as I had in college. I discovered cocaine. It enhanced my gambling experience. One high fed the other, and all I wanted to do was gamble and do coke, and because I had these stimulants, I needed something to come down from that high, and marijuana served that purpose.

Although I was fun to be around and had many friends, often partying and going to clubs, I felt oddly isolated by my cross-addictions. I would be out at the clubs with friends, where we would have tables with bottle service with women surrounding us, yet all I could think of was gambling. I was bored at the club and could only think of getting that high. The addiction became so overwhelming that I would lie to my friends and tell them I was leaving the party to go meet up with other girls. In fact, I was going home to be alone, gamble on the party poker website, use cocaine, and play online poker for hours and hours until the sun came up the next morning and I could continue gambling on sports that came on the next day.

I let the addiction control my behavior and my life. I was completely incapable of having normal relationships, and I compensated by working nonstop and chasing the dollar so I could continue to support and feed my addictions.

At the height of the sickness of my addiction, I was in Atlantic City gambling at the blackjack table. I'd been playing for hours, drinking and doing cocaine. I felt like I was going to be sick, so I left my chips at the table and ran to the bathroom. I couldn't get there in time, so I ended up vomiting on my shirt near the entrance to the bathroom. Although I had a room at the casino, I didn't bother going upstairs to change. I couldn't stop gambling. Instead, I turned my shirt inside out, put it back on, and continued to play at the blackjack table for another three hours. This powerful story illustrates the depth of my gambling addiction.

A MOVE WEST

It took me years to clean up my act. When I did, though, I found myself in the midst of a new opportunity that led me to leave New York City and head west. Four years after 9/11 and still in New York City, things were looking up for me. I'd started going to Gamblers Anonymous (GA) and had gotten clean from most of my addictions—a story that will come later in this book. One day, clear-headed as ever, I found myself calling on E*TRADE Financial to see if I could drum up some sales. The senior vice president of HR told me that she didn't have any business in New Jersey or New York but that there was a huge opportunity in Sandy, Utah, and that they needed to hire two hundred financial service reps in the next three weeks.

I felt like it was divine intervention. After all, I only knew one person outside of the metropolitan area who was in staffing, and she happened to be in Utah, and we had worked together at Hall Kinion years before. I'd always known I would follow in my father's footsteps and be an entrepreneur, and this was the door that seemed to be opening this opportunity. Since the company I was working for didn't want any business outside the New York/New Jersey area, I called her up to see if she was interested. We worked all weekend on putting a bid together and submitted it that Sunday night, and the next day, I received a call from E*TRADE accepting the bid. We had just over three weeks to fill over two hundred financial services positions. I took my two-week vacation from my current position at the time to head to Salt Lake City and dive into the project, and we nailed it. We filled all two hundred positions on time and under budget. Because we were successful, we landed additional E*TRADE business in Alpharetta, Georgia; Tampa, Florida; and Jersey City, New Jersey. We filled eight hundred positions in just one year, all while I was still working my full-time job in New York.

Eventually, my friend who I was working for at the New York company got into a dispute with the owner of that company, which ended up in court, where he was unceremoniously fired. He had a one-year noncompete, which kept him from working in the same business for a while. I, in turn, had a six-month noncompete, so I continued to work at that company for six more months and resigned to align our noncompete periods. Together, we had a plan: after our noncompetes were up, we were going to go into business together.

In the meantime, with my encouragement, my contact out in Utah was leveraging all the success we had with E*TRADE to start her own company—Parallel HR—and I offered to help. I had six months to kill. I moved out there for what was supposed to be six months, and I landed a large account right off the bat. We started filling a lot of jobs and really doing well. We engaged in discussions for me to stay, and an offer was made that was basically equivalent to a fifty-fifty split. Did I want to go into business with her at Parallel HR or stay with the plan and go into business with my childhood friend back in NYC? That was the dilemma I had before me.

In the end and as is typical with a gambling addict—even one in recovery—my decision came down to money and numbers. My best friend was offering me a 30 percent share of the company we were going to open together in

New York—after all, he had four more years of experience and contacts—and my Utah contact was offering me 50 percent. In my mind of chasing the dollar at every turn, it wasn't really much of a decision for me. I needed to follow the money.

For weeks, I dreaded having to tell my good friend. I would now have to break the news to him that everything we had planned and talked about for years would now not be happening because I decided to move to Utah. This decision changed the entire trajectory of my life. Sometimes I wonder how life would have been different. What if I took the job with my buddy in New York City like we had planned? However, over the years I have learned that what-ifs only drain our energy. I've found it better to focus on the present and lessons learned from the past.

FROM LOST TO HERE

I have been clean from gambling since June of 2005. I still attend GA meetings, not only to work on myself but to help others in despair whose clarity is still more raw. I realize I've always had a classic addictive personality, prone to mania and driven to extremes. From scooping up change on a New Jersey freeway to landing million-dollar accounts to running marathons to climbing Mount Kilimanjaro (more to come on that), I've been on a lifelong search for the rush that comes from winning. In a way, I'm still on that search.

Quitting gambling was the right thing to do, but in the aftermath of the decision, I felt *more* empty on the inside because I was forced to deal with my emotional reality, not hide from it behind my addiction. I didn't grow up in an affectionate household and didn't understand emotional intelligence, so coping with *feelings*—whatever those were—was foreign at first. It was so foreign, in fact, that I didn't want to do it, so I jumped into other addictive behavior. I began running marathons and fundraising obsessively. I made poor personnel decisions as a leader in my business and was constantly surrounded by drama. I became involved in a never-ending lawsuit with my ex-business partner who cofounded Parallel HR, and the turmoil from that situation left me feeling angry, alone, and isolated. All those stories will come later in this book, but here's the bottom line: even though I stopped gambling years ago, the feeling of isolation that accompanies addictive behavior—whether it's betting, drinking, drugs, working too much, binging on social media, or a number of other possibilities—still left me feeling alone and empty inside.

However, over the past couple of years, I have truly come to see myself as a human in recovery, an entrepreneur, a philanthropist, and just a much better person all around.

Yes, I'm successful professionally, but I'm also successful personally. I now meditate. I exercise. I volunteer in healthy doses. I'm manifesting my future, and I'm finding the fulfillment I never knew was possible. I'm writing this book in the hope that I can help you do the same. It's never too late to change your reality, and I am the perfect example of this.

ENTREPRENEURSHIP AND ADDICTION OFTEN GO HAND IN HAND

You may not be addicted to gambling, drugs, or alcohol, but if you're an entrepreneur, or high-performing individual, you may have at least *a piece* of an addictive personality. It may sound provocative, but there's truth there. Are you chasing money? Power? Success? Acceptance? Are you addicted to work? Do you struggle with the same highs and lows? Do you feel isolated?

The first thing I did when I arrived in Utah, on the second day I was there, was find the nearest Gamblers Anonymous meeting. I didn't even have a car yet, so I took a cab up to the VA (Veterans Administration) where the meeting was being held. There were fewer than ten people in attendance, and although I was surrounded by like-minded people, I still felt alone. I felt that way in my business too. As an entrepreneur, it can be hard to find the right people to talk to, even if those around you have good intentions. It can be difficult to talk to your employees if you have issues with your personal life or your business because you may feel that conversation could seem unprofessional or be seen as a sign of weakness. You might be able to talk to your family, and they may even *try* to understand, but unless they own a business, they will never fully comprehend what you're going through.

So what do you do? Instead, you focus on making every dollar you can and building your company not just because you're promoting your product or service but also because people are counting on you for their livelihoods. Entrepreneurship comes with a particular pressure and, often, an impulse toward the extreme, but it doesn't have to. I just didn't know any better.

In the following chapters, I will lead you through a series of steps along the path to self-discovery. Along with recounting some of my personal experiences, I will also examine both the good and the bad that can come from your entrepreneurial drive and ambition. Ultimately, I'll show that achieving positive transformation in your life is not only possible but within reach. If you're feeling stuck and are looking to get out of your own way, I encourage you to stay with me. If you are interested in how I changed a miserable life into one of fulfillment, please come along for the journey.

THE TURNING POINT

You can't force an alcoholic to go to Alcoholics Anonymous. You can't force a drug addict to go to Narcotics Anonymous. Nobody could have forced me to go to Gamblers Anonymous, and if they had tried, I would have resisted. Similarly, I'm not forcing any ideas or strategies upon you. I know how that ends up, especially when faced with an entrepreneurial ego—one that, by the way, I still share but that I do a much better job of keeping in check.

What's the path forward, then? How do you begin to open your mind and see that a different life is truly possible? It wasn't about changing my mindset or practicing positive thinking for me at the time. Instead, it was about finding that moment of clarity.

Maybe this is you too?

CHAPTER ONE

THE MOMENT OF CLARITY

The term "moment of clarity" is common in the addiction and recovery world. Simply put, it means the moment when your truth finally breaks through the deep layers of your denial. Before a moment of clarity, addicts—or anyone facing a struggle of any kind—often feel stuck. You feel like nothing is clicking. Maybe you're in a rut with negative personal habits, in a job you don't love, in a relationship that's not the best, or in some other situation that is dragging you down. Although you want to get out from under your stressor—and maybe have even tried in the past—it doesn't seem like there's any escape. You feel stuck. You haven't taken enough (or the right) action to move forward, and it can feel like you simply exist in your private, predictable hell.

Then, the aha moment comes. Something happens that opens your eyes to a new perspective, and you start believing. That belief turns into curiosity, and that curiosity turns into action. The action starts to happen when you're surrounding yourself with more of whatever originally got you to that moment of clarity. Moments of clarity are personal and different for everyone, so there is no mold. A commonality, though, is where you find yourself after one occurs: in a place of empowerment coupled with vulnerability, ready to break through whatever is holding you back.

Ironically, my moment of clarity came thirteen years ago on my way to *another* Massachusetts Thanksgiving.

GAINING NEW PERSPECTIVE

As I got into the car with my brother, preparing for another three-hour drive to our annual Thanksgiving holiday getaway a few states away, I appeared to have everything together. I was the director of business development for a successful staffing company in New York City where I made six figures. I wore nice suits and nice watches, had a nice apartment, and kept a busy social life, but nobody knew I was gambling every day, multiple times a day. I chased the high so often that I looked for opportunities everywhere. When my friends and I would go to lunch, we'd play a game we called credit card roulette with each of us throwing in our credit card and telling the waitress to pick one at random to see who paid the entire bill. It seemed fun and I loved to laugh, but inside, I was miserable and constantly distracted and in turmoil.

"Turn that off," my brother said as I switched the radio dial to sports radio in preparation for our journey. Since my uncle gave me my first gambling card twenty years before when we went to Thanksgiving, I had always paid more attention to the football games on TV than to my extended family, even though I only saw them once a year. The drive there was no different. I wanted to detach and learn everything I could about the upcoming games by listening to sports radio.

"What are you talking about?" I asked him. "I need to make my Fantasy Football team selections and need the latest updates."

"No," he said. "I can't listen to sports radio anymore. I stopped gambling. I started going to GA, and I don't want to listen to this right now. Let's just listen to music."

I walked the line between being annoyed and being agitated. "Are you serious?" I fired back. "Give me a break. Okay, so you're never going to listen to sports radio again for the rest of your life? That's absurd."

We went back and forth, as brothers do, and I realized I wasn't going to win. Plus, he was driving, so I relented, which, at the time, was a big deal for me. I was addicted to sports radio because it fueled my betting. I went to sleep listening to it every single night and waking up to it every single morning, so I was pissed. But I changed the station and turned on classic rock. Then, gradually, this little action allowed my perspective to begin changing.

I realized I wasn't thinking about gambling or teams or scores or spreads or odds. The music was soothing, and my mind wasn't racing a million miles a minute. I felt calm and clear-headed. It felt weird and unlike myself, but I *liked* it. When we arrived, I told my brother I was glad we had listened to music and it was such a relaxing ride. It was a little change, but it made a big difference. I thought to myself, *What did this GA do to my brother?* Even though I was still skeptical about the whole thing, it brought up a curiosity, and I wanted to check it out, not because I thought I had a problem but just to see how it changed him.

"When we get home, I'm going to come to a meeting," I told him. "I just need to know what they've done to my brother."

So I went to a meeting upon our return, and since walking into that first meeting thirteen years ago, I have never made another bet and have attended meetings ever since.

ARE YOU LOOKING FOR YOUR MOMENT OF CLARITY?

If you are a type A person, who often finds yourself reaching for extremes, I realize you are probably a lot like I was riding in that car next to my brother. It may seem like you have everything under control on the outside, and others believe that you do. On the inside, though, you might feel overwhelmed, stuck, and lost. If you've been trying to reach a breakthrough by taking deep breaths or repeating affirmations, you might be waiting a while. Instead, I believe you've got to come to *your* moment of clarity—a moment that peaks the curiosity of thinking or living a different way.

For me, reaching my moment of clarity was about overcoming the fear of stopping something forever. NEVER is an incredibly powerful word, for anyone, especially for an addict. I did something I normally wouldn't do—not listen to sports radio, even for a short amount of time— and I saw how it felt. That small act opened up a curiosity, which led to a new perspective that eventually took me out of my perpetual state of mental anguish.

Your moment of clarity will undoubtedly look different than mine, but it starts from the same place: a willingness to peel back the mask you are letting represent you. That mask could be one of a successful entrepreneur, a wife, a husband, a department head, or a parent, and I am sure there are many other examples. Whatever mask you are wearing, there needs to be self-acknowledgment that you might be feeling completely different on the inside than what you are representing on the outside. Once you acknowledge this, try opening your mind to a different way of thinking and expand your reality, even if it's small at first. It could be listening to a daily motivational podcast, trying meditation, exercising more consistently, reading a book you might not normally consider reading, or whatever other outlet provides you with new information on your struggle. This is what led me to find a sense of calm, allowing my mind to stop racing and for me to stop prejudging everything and consider a different way to live. Unless you take this first step, nothing is going to change. You'll still be in your bubble of negativity or struggle, surrounded by your sphere of people who may not fully support healthy habits or understand what you're going through.

Freeing yourself from that uncomfortable bubble begins with opening your mind to different messages around you. Not everything will resonate, but one day, something will. If you try to listen to different voices and different styles of communicating, you might be surprised what you'll find. If it's difficult and you find yourself automatically saying no to a question or an opportunity, consider taking a step back and asking if it would be so bad to approach situations in a different way. I attribute this very thought process to major shifts I have been able to make in my life.

LESSONS LEARNED

I hated my first GA meeting. I looked around the room at the smattering of people and felt superior to them all. Single people. Married people. Young people. Old people. A mailman. A gym teacher. A mother. A grandfather. They all looked like degenerates to me. I looked around the room and felt like I had nothing in common with any of them. At the end of the meeting, I started speaking with one of the senior guys there and a GA sponsor. After listening to my logic, he got right in my face, yelling passionately about my belief system. (After all, we were in New Jersey.) He was strongly disagreeing with me and was so close to me that spit was flying from his mouth, landing all over my face. I thought he was crazy—that they all were. I judged them. I actually despised them. To say I felt iffy about the whole GA thing would be an understatement.

They asked two things of me: to not gamble tomorrow and to come back next meeting. With their urging and support, I went back the following week. Then I went back again. And again. Slowly, after half-assing then eventually wholeheartedly working the twelve steps, I realized I had more in common with every single person in that room than I did with the majority of people I had thought were my friends for years.

I found that clarity from doing one simple thing: taking action. Even though I got to that first GA meeting with a chip on my shoulder, I got there. If you want results, you have to *act* when an opportunity for a new perspective presents itself. Be curious. Feeling stuck or isolated is a mind game, and the first step to beating it is to make a move.

What might that look like for you?

CHAPTER TWO

JUST. DO. IT.

Did your moment of clarity spike your confidence or at least pique a realization that you can make things happen? If so, you might be asking: Now what? Is there a roadmap to find the next step?" The simple answer is that it's less about having a map and more about having the courage to hit the gas in the first place. To get yourself out there and create change, you need to open your mind and take action.

Taking action can be difficult because we're often trapped in our own bubbles of negativity. We coast along, living in a perception molded by friends, family, coworkers, and society. And why not, right? Taking the path of least resistance is a natural reaction. Making a change, especially a life-altering change, feels difficult, heavy, and unnatural. That's okay, but it's just not true. Change is easy, and everyone has the power to do it. It may take time and courage, but it is actually quite easy. Once you allow yourself to realize that things could be better in your life, you can open your mind to different messages, new communication techniques, and information that will resonate differently and bring opportunities for you to move forward.

The opposite is also true: if you struggle to maintain happiness or some sort of balance in your life, surrounding yourself with like-minded people only adds to that struggle. For example, when I was gambling, I used to think I had so many awesome, cool, fun friends. It was only when I stopped gambling and they all disappeared that I realized that most of them were not friends at all. They were simply people to gamble and party with. I never would have come to this realization if I hadn't taken action after changing that radio station on that ride to Thanksgiving all those years ago.

Prior to that impactful car ride, I had never admitted to anyone that I was addicted to gambling, including myself. To me, it was just a way of life. When my brother unknowingly gave me that abrupt realization, it was the crack I needed to open the door to making that change. Attending the meeting was the second step—the action. Listening to others in the meeting was the third step. I didn't want to be there, and they knew it. Still, they were straight with me. They followed up. They called. They supported. They didn't let me quit.

Gradually, I accepted that I was indeed an addict and let the process of the program take its course. It wasn't easy. They felt like tiny, baby steps, but they were steps. I listened to the group and worked the twelve-step program with everyone else. I did not necessarily have to accept everything that I was learning, but I at least had to be open to exploring these ways, have a curiosity around them, and show up.

I fell into meditation in this manner—something that has served as a peaceful escape, helping calm my thoughts and focus my mind in a positive direction. I had never considered meditation as a solution or even temporary escape, but I got curious and dipped in a toe. At first, the type of meditation I looked at, transcendental meditation, was way too intense for me. So I found a different meditation that resonated with me and allowed me to ease into it at a comfortable pace. From that quick moment of decision in my life, I learned it makes such a difference to keep an open mind and to be curious, especially if you are in a rut. The lesson I learned was simple: you don't have to believe everything about something before trying it! Just jump in, try not to prejudge, and let your guard down. Don't overthink it. This process starts by stepping out of your comfort zone, and once you do that, miraculous things can happen.

RUNNING FOR A CAUSE

I took my own advice to heart with a move west. Just prior to my move to Salt Lake City, I caught a bug to run a marathon. My brother had run a couple in the past, and I always had that competitive older-brother mindset of wanting to one-up him. Although I had never run one before, I decided to enter the New York City Marathon. Organizers use a lottery system to select entrants for the popular race, and through a little random good luck, I was selected. With the ensuing move to Salt Lake City and total lack of marathon experience, I had no idea if I'd be able to make the event. I packed up and decided to just figure it out later.

The second week in Salt Lake City, I made a fortuitous visit to, of all places, a pizza shop. On a wall in the entryway, I saw a flyer for Team In Training, a chapter of the Leukemia & Lymphoma Society (LLS). Team In Training focuses on training people for marathons while the participants raise funds for LLS. Team In Training covers entry into a marathon, and in return, you raise a certain amount of money for them.

I was already looking for people to train with, and I loved the mission of Team In Training. Building up for an event that big is difficult to do alone, so I needed some companionship to pile on training miles. I attended one of their meetings, and there on the spot, I decided to go for it.

Although I didn't have anyone in my immediate family who suffered from leukemia, I had known two people in high school who had contracted the disease and tragically passed away at very young ages. One was a class valedictorian who passed away in college. The other was an avid, successful wrestler. I also knew many others affected by different forms of cancer. As I heard stories from the others in the group, I became even more aware of how far-reaching the impact of the terrible disease truly is and the toll it can take on those affected and their families. Immediately, I signed up and started fundraising.

Besides the leukemia connection, the Team In Training opportunity appealed to me on a fundamental level too. I always volunteer when I can, and I like to give back. I dove into the marathon routine, training with groups of participants on weekends and following a focused running schedule during the week. The fundraising required serious commitment. I wrote letters requesting donations for the cause, raised $5,000, and traveled back to New York for the marathon. Running the New York Marathon was an amazing experience. The entire experience was invigorating. I was hooked.

I ran three more marathons over the next four years, all through Team In Training. I competed in the Salt Lake City marathon and also traveled to Vancouver, Canada, and Anchorage, Alaska, to run those marathons as well. We trained and participated together, and raised a great deal of money for LLS. It was a life-changing experience and helped shape my focus on paying it forward however I could. It was selfish in a sense because it made me feel good about myself and also had the added benefit of helping others. All the time and effort involved was the ideal antidote for my post-gambling life.

TAKING ACTION: MORE RUNNING, MORE FUNDRAISING

A common characteristic of all addictions is the amount of time they consume. As an addict, I spent about 75 percent of every day doing something involving feeding my gambling addiction. When I wasn't gambling, I would be researching sporting events that I could gamble on. I would travel to horse tracks, casinos, card games, and other places where I could place bets. I even weaved gambling around work meetings in New York City. Before or after a meeting, I made side trips to the bank to withdraw money before speeding across town to pay off my bookie. I was so addicted to the rush that I just kept doing it. It wasn't as much about winning or losing. Instead, I was driven by continuing to chase that rush, that high I would get every time I placed a bet. It was a feeling of pure adrenaline that I could not duplicate any other way. Frankly, it was manic, sick behavior.

During and after GA meetings, though, I suddenly had a lot of extra time on my hands—75 percent more time, to be exact. Many addicts search for new distractions or find new hobbies or different friends to fill the void. When you are battling through addiction, you try to change your behavior patterns. All of a sudden, one is presented with a lot of extra time in their life to fill. Filling that extra time with positive activities and positive people is very important, and running did that for me. The camaraderie and support of the group was a huge step forward in my recovery. I opened up more, connected with many amazing people, and felt good about raising money for such an important cause.

Unfortunately during this time, I injured my back and had to undergo back surgery. After I had surgery, I was so amped up that I started running again. I jumped back in a little too soon, and it led to yet another surgery. After that, I took a one-year break to recover but still had an insatiable mental hunger to prove to myself that I could still run a marathon after two back surgeries. So I did that one last marathon for LLS in Vancouver, Canada, and it was a big one. The event was unforgettable, like all the rest, but I struggled physically and mentally to get through it. Sadly, I knew it would be my last.

I still stayed connected with the Leukemia & Lymphoma Society and attended several of their events and some of their galas, supporting other efforts over the years. Then, three years after my last marathon, in 2016 and out of the blue, I received a surprise call from LLS congratulating me for being nominated for their Man & Woman of the Year Award. This award was given to the man and woman in every state who raised the most money in a ten-week national fundraising blitz. I was to compete with seven other men and women in Utah.

My initial reaction was one of resistance. In fact, that had long been my natural reaction to most things. I argued with my brother when he wanted to turn off my sports radio—resistance. I balked at confronting my addiction—resistance. When I finally went to meetings, I didn't want to listen to anyone there—resistance. Whenever someone even told me to do something—well, you guessed it, I resisted. I became combative and argumentative, and I never lost an argument! Now, a charity was urging me into another commitment that I didn't have "time" for. I mean, I had a business to run, and that was more important than anything. At least, these were my initial thoughts.

I replied that I simply had too much going on with my business and would not be able to participate. After rethinking that initial feeling and response, I agreed to at least meet with LLS staff to learn more about the event. It turned out the fundraising was in recognition of their Boy and Girl of the Year—a four- and five-year-old in Utah who were currently undergoing chemotherapy treatments. I remained hesitant and delivered a litany of excuses to myself and reasons for them as to why I couldn't do it. Why had my name come up in the first place? How was I nominated for this? Hadn't I done enough? Still, I told them I'd think about it.

I went back and forth on the decision, staring at pictures of the four and-five-year-old kids with their cute smiles, and my heart eventually won out. I didn't know what I was getting myself into, but I agreed to participate. Quickly, I put a team together to support these efforts. If I was going to do this, I thought, I was going to do it right. My team had a kick-off meeting, and I followed up with fundraising events in New York and Salt Lake City. The Salt Lake City event, in particular, was a large foodie gathering. Five local chefs volunteered their time, and we had a DJ and open bar. Over one hundred people attended, and we had the Girl of the Year call in from her family's home to speak to the whole group on a large-screen TV. It was an inspiring, uplifting moment. All told, in ten weeks of fundraising, my team and I were able to raise $75,000, and although I wanted to win Man of the Year badly (because, clearly, I have a bit of a competitive streak and certainly an ego), instead, I came in second place, with the winner being a Hodgkin's survivor himself who was able to raise $85,000. I quickly checked my sour grapes at the door.

More numbers came in, and two of the amazing women raised $100,000 each! Among eight of us, we raised $585,000 in ten weeks. It was the most money raised in the competition and broke all Utah group fundraising records.

Throughout the fundraising, I grew close to the Boy and Girl of the Year. I really started caring on a personal level about them and their families and admired how brave they were. I wondered if I would be as brave in their situation, and I wanted to do something special for them. On the night of the event finale, I brought the Boy and Girl of the Year giant stuffed animals and presented them on stage. The kids' smiles were priceless and meant more to me than anything else. I don't have kids of my own, but they have a special place in my heart. And the best news? Both the Boy and Girl of the Year are now in remission.

In spite of the huge success, I initially was upset and let down that I did not win. Because of my skewed mindset and how my brain worked, I looked at things the wrong way. After raising $75,000 I actually thought I failed. I was pissed and depressed. Looking back, it was such an odd reaction. It took me a day or two to shake out of it and realize I was being absurd, but thanks to the work that I have done on myself, I can now recognize that hang-up and correct it much quicker than I used to. At the end of the day, we raised a huge chunk of money for a great cause and stood by two special kids. It was a great accomplishment and something I'll be proud of for the rest of my life. I'm still thankful to everyone involved. You can't raise that much money and coordinate that many events alone; it takes dedicated support and a drive to succeed. And as a bonus, I developed several strong friendships throughout the process that wouldn't have happened if I hadn't taken the leap. Prior to the event, I felt down and stuck again in my life. I was angry at the world and just was not productive, personally or with my business. The LLS opportunity happened at exactly the right time. All I had to do was take that initial step of saying, "Yes, I'll do it," and others followed and supported all the effort it took.

LESSONS LEARNED

You may have similar opportunities for growth in your life that you simply can't see because you feel stuck and can't transcend your own state of mind, which happened to me several times. I couldn't get out of my own way, and you may feel the same. Maybe you concede defeat or say no before really looking at what's there. That's why they call it a leap of faith. There's a hesitation before the jump. The action you take doesn't have to be a dramatic event or grand gesture. Small victories are equally significant because they open doors that would have otherwise remained closed, perhaps indefinitely. The smallest action can have the biggest impact.

At the onset of the fundraising event, I was skeptical because I had no idea how I would make it happen. Now, I'm content in the knowledge that we don't always need to know how it will all work out. It is often better if we don't have a crystal ball of the road in front of us and instead simply follow our intuition, trust the process, and change our mindsets to accept and embrace what the road brings, even if setbacks are inevitable. Overcoming those roadblocks is where the lessons are truly learned.

CHAPTER THREE

THE CLASSIC STRUGGLE

The journey to overcoming addictive behaviors starts with a moment of clarity, is followed by immediate action, and—almost inevitably—is followed by an early stumble or two or three. It's what I refer to as the classic evolution through addiction.

Early setbacks are opportunities for growth, resilience, and greater self-awareness, but they don't always feel that way. Addiction is very much an emotional disease. It can lead to a physical reliance on substance, but at its core, it is emotional. When you do something for so long in a particular way or with a particular person, it's difficult to change that habit. Are you addicted to spending all your time at the office, always obsessed with the next sale or the next milestone for your business? Are you obsessed with achieving a goal, and it's affecting your personal life and relationships? When you try to change those habits, you may miss a step. It's easy to feel defeated and to question whether or not you've made the right decision. A new habit of uncertainty can take over, stalling progress toward recovery.

It's easy to convince yourself life isn't any better without the addiction, and it can feel comfortable slipping back into old habits. A positive mindset is difficult to keep when you haven't addressed the root issue and don't feel good on the inside. You might have stopped what you were doing and eliminated a bad habit, but you can still feel static. When you don't feel like you are making any progress, it can be easy to simply give up—or, in my case, replace one unhealthy behavior with another.

ONE ADDICTION FEEDS ANOTHER

At times during recovery, you might look back and think you had more fun inside the addiction, although you know the reality is that the ramifications of these actions had very negative lasting results. Similarly, at times in your career, you might look back and think you had more fun when you took your eye off the ball and focused on building a new idea or product—even a failed one—outside your core business. In both cases, though, the reality can be quite different than what you envisioned. The majority of times, it can create more challenges in life. People end up not having more fun or more success. It can be frightening to teeter so vulnerably on the edge, trying to disassociate from your long-held feelings with no idea what's on the other side.

The same happened to me. Even though I stopped gambling, I made my situation worse with cross-addictions. I brought drug use into the mix, especially on weekends. I could function well enough during the week, but I still smoked pot all the time, and weekends became one long haze. I was treading water.

What did it matter if I'd stopped gambling if I was simply replacing one addiction with another? Was I doing what was best for me, or was I just turning to another comfort? When you step away from addiction—whatever that may be—and move in a different direction, it's essential that you work at it, maintaining reflection, understanding, and self-awareness. I didn't expect that part of recovery, and I wasn't mature enough to embrace it. I wasn't in a place to put in that type of work for several years after stopping the gambling.

Many people place great importance on finding out the "why" of addiction. They enter a program with a need to unearth the origin of their problem. I, however, didn't need to know why I did it. The complicated, therapeutically or medically explained reason? Nah, I just had no interest in that. Instead, I just wanted to stop feeling so miserable, manic, and lonely inside. I wanted to grow as a person and move forward. However, I couldn't do any of that until I looked inside and asked myself how I wanted to live. How could I gain control of my actions and my behavior? I realized what was important to me and took steps to get there.

My initial reaction was to replace gambling with something positive. Your positive distraction could be meditation, yoga, reading, rock climbing—there are a million healthy behaviors you could choose. I chose running. Although I replaced a negative behavior with one I felt was positive, I still wasn't balanced internally, so just like with gambling, I took it to the extreme. I ran a ton of miles, and even while I was doing that, I still went home and smoked a ton of pot. Looking back, I can see that I didn't understand what was truly healthy for me, both physically and mentally. Still, I took what I thought would be the quickest route that would leave me the most fulfilled.

It took years for me to realize that while I thought I was getting healthier by replacing gambling with something positive, like running or fundraising, I wasn't. I just had new addictions. They were better, healthier addictions, for sure. Inevitably, though, when I couldn't run anymore after back surgery, it left a gaping hole. This realization was a setback to recovery, but it was also an opportunity to grow. I discovered it's easy to convince yourself that by doing something positive, you are eliminating all traces of the negative. However, doing an extreme amount of "the new positive" has its own drawbacks.

When I stopped running, for example, I fell back into my old, familiar rut. *What the hell am I going to do with all of this newly found time?* I wondered. The void was the same. Outwardly, I looked like I had it all together—a hallmark of my life as an addict. I'd been in Utah for five years, and my life seemed wonderful. I was continuing to build a flourishing business, I was fit from running multiple marathons, and it felt good to give back through my fundraising work. Throughout all the outward successes, though, I struggled with inward turmoil related to my personal life. Being from New Jersey, I didn't know many people in Utah, and it was difficult to find people I truly could trust and confide in. It was challenging to really connect on a deep level with friends and even harder to date. All the relationships I had were surface level. I felt alone all the time, even in crowds.

My negativity festered. I was continually self-deprecating, constantly beating myself up inside with thoughts of not being good enough or of being a failure. Slowly, these feelings began to take more of a presence in my life, and I had no idea how to deal with the negative thoughts. They are formidable opponents. Traditionally, men have an image of being stoic, tough, and ready to handle anything thrown their way, but that's a bullshit image. I couldn't handle it.

I was very uncomfortable opening up to anyone about it, so I just locked it all in. I would go out with people and have fun, smiling and joking, but all the while, I was hiding torment on the inside. It was easy for me to hide it because I'd done it for so long. No one suspected I had that much pain. This "one step forward, two steps back" scenario is common in the world of recovery. It's going to happen. However, it's part of the journey—a healthy and productive part for me. It might not feel like it, but the classic struggle is one of the most important steps on your path to finally achieving fulfillment. The more it happens, the easier your journey will eventually be. As one becomes more vulnerable and authentic, you get stronger and your periods of funk get shorter. The light can be difficult to see under the weight of all the negativity, but it is there.

EVOLVING FROM THE INSIDE OUT

To reach that light, creating a routine has been a critical driving factor. For me, an exercise, podcast, and meditation routine has helped leave me more fulfilled and in line with my emotions. These practices make me feel healthy and give me a positive attitude and mindset. When I get away from my routine and stop working out, for example, it takes so much longer to mentally get back into the groove. Scheduling activities helps keep me on track, break through the mental blocks, and return to form. Listening to positive podcasts strengthens my mind. Meditation allows me to examine my soul. I understand this about me because I've gained self-awareness—the result of many mistakes and missteps along the way.

After some rough roads and more than my share of doubting, I've learned the most important ingredients to achieving fulfillment in your life is to keep an open mind to new things, to take care of yourself physically and emotionally, and most importantly, to love yourself. When we roll through life's ups and downs, the one thing we can control is our own physical and mental health. The emotional struggles inherent with addiction, death, sickness, and other hurdles are challenging, yes. Without a solid foundation, though, they can be crippling and lead to more pain and self-destruction.

LESSONS LEARNED

If you are not happy internally and don't appreciate yourself, love yourself, and clearly understand what fulfills you, it's incredibly difficult to fully be there for yourself or for others. Some say finding our own happiness is the key, but happiness is a relative term. I think fulfillment is the better illustrator of my point. If you can do all the things necessary to treat yourself well, you will be more present. You'll be a better friend, leader, spouse, family member, or colleague, able to love and communicate on a deeper, more meaningful level.

On the flip side, if you don't maintain your sense of self, it's easy to end up isolated, apprehensive, and even slide into depression. You need to consistently love yourself first and not be afraid to feed that love in whatever healthy way that works best for you. I have found exercising, listening to positive podcasts or music that lights you up, meditating, surrounding yourself with positive people, and looking for solutions instead of excuses, all help keep the mind headed in a positive direction and clear of negativity. Without a healthy dose, we end up with nonproductive distractions and negative energy that weighs us down and blocks progress toward mental growth, halting our ability to fulfill our potential.

Remember, you will encounter roadblocks along the way. Expect them. Be aware of your surroundings every day, and adapt to what is best for you. Make the difficult choices that allow you to avoid falling into traps that seem to lie in wait around every corner. Put roadblocks in place that help you stay on track. Know that the stumbles along the way are temporary and can be taken as lessons learned. My own stumbles brought me to the self-awareness I have today, and now I know I can't love others and be at my highest level of being until I love and take care of myself first.

I was able to overcome my setbacks by turning to self-examination. For me, a big part of my self-examination was focused on something that had plagued me in one way or another since that Thanksgiving when I was ten years old: my relationship with money.

CHAPTER FOUR

WHAT IS MONEY ANYWAY?

Often, we fling headlong through life, meeting hurdles and roadblocks all the while. Those obstacles can slow us down, make us stumble, and even push us backward. Opportunities to learn and grow come with adversity, however, and we create new relationships or nurture old ones. What we do with opportunity makes us who we are.

Relationships take place most often with other people, but one of the most intimate relationships entrepreneurs, business owners, and for that matter, most people have is with money. We are driven to be the best, and for many, that is measured by the almighty dollar. This stage in the journey is about examining the role money plays in our lives. The exchange of currency and accumulation of wealth is so woven into the fabric of our society that we don't often step back and examine its role in our decisions. There is great value, however, in looking at money objectively, with an almost childlike innocence—but it's not always that easy.

I think most people feel like money can make you, but it can also destroy you. For as long as I can remember, I based every decision in my life around money. It was usually a cost-benefit assessment I conducted in my own mind. I was always concerned with accumulating *more* than the next person—fancier suits, nicer cars, a shinier watch, multiple houses, etc. All things that, from my current vantage point, I can see meant absolutely nothing in the big picture. Back then, though, I couldn't see it. Every decision I made in my life was based on the desire to have more of the almighty dollar.

The majority of the time, those decisions didn't really work out for me.

MORE MONEY, MORE PROBLEMS

Looking back, my money chase started at home. I was fortunate enough to grow up in a middle-class family in New Jersey with a father who was an entrepreneur. I believed from a young age that how much money I had determined how successful of a person I was. My dad worked constantly. He was always busting his ass at work, so that's all I knew. The downside was he was never really around because he was always working. The upside? He imparted a strong work ethic I still have today. However, it was not a fulfilled life, and I carried on that habit as well: all work and no play or, sometimes in my case, too much play. It was a life of extremes.

I chased money from the start and, through much of my adult life, never gave much thought to how much I spent on a daily basis. Budgets? Sales? Coupons? No, those weren't me. I've long known how to *make* money, but I never valued it the way it should be. This led to having an adversarial relationship with money. It is something so critical yet so overhyped in society today.

Don't get me wrong. I don't advocate reckless spending. My habits certainly came back to bite me when my business stumbled and some investments went sour. If I ran into financial snags, though, my gambling mentality kicked in. *No worries,* I thought. *I'll make the money back. I'll win again. I'll work harder and longer and close more deals and put my emotional stability to the side so I can make that dollar.*

MONEY AS ROCKET FUEL

I've always been fueled by a specific vision of wealth, and I simply wanted to be rich. I thought that once I had loads of money, everything else would come. I'd get the girl. I'd retire at fifty, buy a yacht, and sail it around the world—everything we see in the movies. I would actually repeat this to anyone who would listen. I wanted to be far more successful than my friends and have more money than everyone. I thought that's what happiness was. It was a ridiculous scenario I made up in my head, but I was so misaligned that it drove me and gave me that rush similar to gambling.

Because I never treated money with respect, nearly every decision I made where money was the driving factor was a decision that ended up going south. I've made many money-driven decisions throughout my entire life with disastrous results. Some of these decisions ended up in lawsuits costing more in legal fees than the value of the actual disputes. Hundreds of thousands of dollars down the drain, along with lost time and what seemed like never-ending mental stress. I've been left emotionally destroyed and confused about my purpose in life.

Emotions and money are strangely tethered. It seems the two are easy to keep at arm's length, but there is an irresistible attraction between them. For example, a friend approached me several years ago and asked to borrow $2,000. Because I had the money and he was a friend, I agreed without a second thought. He said he'd pay me back in a week, after all, so I thought nothing of it.

A week passed, and he didn't pay me back. Then another week. Then another. As six months passed, it was the only thing I could think about. I was running a $5 million company and was obsessed over $2,000 because I felt as though I was being screwed over and betrayed—a feeling that's always left me pissed off with a vengeful, fueled feeling. No one was going to screw me: *Oh hell no.* I knew enough about how leverage can work for you in business, so I did the same thing in this situation. After six months of carrying this feeling around with me, I eventually decided to send his girlfriend a message on Facebook about what he did and how he was treating me and the entire situation. As I suspected would happen, based on the positive relationship I had with his girlfriend, I was paid within forty-eight hours in full.

Looking back, I realize how minor the debacle was in the grand scheme of life, yet I was obsessed about not getting screwed over. It completely consumed me and left me emotionally exhausted. I made it my mission to get that money back. Nobody was going to screw me. Obviously, it's never pleasant to be taken for that amount of money, but to be that obsessed with it was very unhealthy. I talked about it all the time to other people who were friends with him, playing the victim role. It took over every thought I had, every day. Yes, I eventually got the money back, but did I really win? Probably not, but I learned a very valuable lesson about lending money and what it might lead me to do as all sorts of thoughts ran through my head.

MONEY CAN CREATE A MONSTER

It took a trip to the other side of the world to wake me up. At a business accelerator in Bali called Unconventional Life, some of the other attendees sparked a discussion on the issue of money. At the time, I was going through a lawsuit with my ex-business partner that was incredibly stressful and financially draining. At Unconventional Life, though, I had a breakthrough: I realized money was a trigger in my life and had been the cause of every single problem I'd ever had. I finally recognized the unhealthy, adversarial relationship I had with money. Prior to Bali, I was frustrated, angry, isolated, and just a mess. Every single week, I'd closely examine my business finances to be sure money got where it needed to, checking off every box from employees to overhead to accounting and legal fees. The one year the company lost money, our credit line with Chase Bank was cut off with a balance $280,000. Just like that, the bank termed the credit line into a seven-year loan with a very high interest rate without even consulting with us. It took me an additional five years to pay that off and cost an extra $30,000. Whatever personal money I had went straight into the business just to make payroll. I was barely keeping above water.

I kept my financial situation under the radar, though, shifting personal money around however I could to keep the company financially sound. I borrowed from credit cards, private supporters, and others when I needed to. It was all very similar to the creative financing I concocted to keep gambling: take money from a credit card to keep the bank account full. Use that money to pay the bookie. Funnel my paycheck back to the bank account to repay the credit card. On top of it all, I had a lawsuit hanging over me. I lurched around in a rage, pissed off at the world.

During this time, I had expanded my business back into New York, along with the office I had in India and the one in Salt Lake City. Every time I got near any of the offices, I was in a negative mood before even stepping in the door. *Let's just get shit done so we can make money and pay some damn bills,* was not only my thought process, but it was also my demeanor. I was out to make money, and that's all that mattered. I felt pressure from all sides: a loan I was paying back that I had from buying the company, the credit line that Chase termed into another loan, the standard company expenses, and the lawsuit. Ultimately, that lawsuit started to affect my finances, and I completely lost direction. I wasn't focused on building relationships with my employees and became a hostile boss. I simply couldn't get out of my own way.

To make matters worse, I would go out and spend loads of money on negative habits and experiences just to blow off steam and get out of my own head. I'd go through hundreds of dollars a night getting wasted at strip clubs and then smoking pot and disappearing in a haze. I stopped going to the gym and taking care of myself. I became a ball of anger, hate, and denial, working twelve hours a day, going home, getting high, and eating all night. The same scene repeated itself the next day. And the next week.

When I was in New York City and would walk down the street and someone glanced my way, the first thought in my mind would be, *What the hell are you looking at?* I felt a mix of paranoia and anger, full of negative energy and thoughts. Looking back, it was such a heavy feeling and burden to carry that around all the time. It's not *only* that I didn't want to talk about my financial challenges, but I just didn't want to talk to anyone about any of it *period*.

If someone gave their opinion to me about the business or even asked about it, I would snap at them: "You don't know anything about the business. There's no reason to talk about it." I would constantly snap at the people close to me, telling them, "You won't understand, and you're going to give me advice that doesn't even matter." I would speak harshly, not even thinking about the power of those words and that words do matter and certainly have an impact on other people. I was driven purely by ego, shutting out anyone who wanted to help.

LESSONS LEARNED

Money and anything revolving around it can be an extremely emotional, sensitive issue. What I learned is that it's important to think about it as objectively as possible, as difficult as that can be. Money is a central part of our lives, but we don't typically step back to give it perspective because emotions run high when money is involved. For example, if my payroll department is one day late paying contractors, the contractors' immediate thought is they are being screwed. In reality, perhaps we changed an internal payroll system, and there was a glitch, or a new person on the staff possibly made a mistake. The error could have been caused by any number of reasonable circumstances, but because money is such an emotional issue, it sparks an instant emotional reaction.

As a business owner, I've learned it's critical to keep money in perspective and consider employees' and vendors' emotional engagement. If you lose that outlook, it can put you behind the eight ball in terms of management approaches, mentoring, and working together. If you don't treat money with the value it deserves, it can be difficult to relate to how sensitive it is to others, and I've learned relating to others is the key to not being alone and the key to growth.

CHAPTER FIVE

YOU ARE
NOT ALONE

As people—and especially as entrepreneurs—sometimes we put ourselves in boxes and think nobody understands what we're going through. It's hard to find people to confide in who share the same responsibilities, who understand the life we lead, and who can offer advice during times of crises. This leads to a go-it-alone attitude and ends with feelings of isolation. The solution is one similar to a strategy familiar in the addiction and recovery world: find a support network that is built on the pillars of related ability, support, and accountability. They exist, and having people in your corner makes it that much easier to put up roadblocks. I know because I've lived on both sides and achieved growth and perspective when surrounded by like-minded individuals.

UNEXPECTED CONNECTIONS

In the thick of my gambling addiction, I was convinced no one else could possibly understand what I was going through. I didn't feel comfortable talking to anyone because I felt utterly alone and embarrassed.

I realized how wrong I was at my first Gamblers Anonymous meeting. The meeting took place in a church basement in Fairlawn, New Jersey, with a group of people who, to me, looked about as vibrant as a gloomy, rainy evening. My first impression was that the group was filled with degenerate losers. I was different, I told myself. I was a successful professional. I wore a suit to work every day. I worked in New York City, the mecca. I was on a different level than all of these people. I judged every one of them on sight, and it was all I could do to keep from turning on my heel and walking right out of there.

Then, they started talking. My jaw dropped, and my head nodded in agreement with the personal turmoil they were describing. I could relate to everything being spoken. I sat there, mostly dumbstruck. *Holy shit*, I thought, *I have more in common with these people than anyone else in my life*. That was the point at which I realized I was not alone, not by a long shot. We were all completely different people, grew up in different environments, and had drastically different lives. In spite of that, we had so much in common through addiction and its side effects. The inner pain and suffering we were all going through was drastically similar.

Prior to attending GA meetings, I didn't want to open up to other people because I felt like I was consistently complaining, that no one could relate, and that I would be judged. I heard myself say the same thing over and over, and it frustrated me. I wanted myself to shut up. But when I started to let my guard down and drop the facade, I had a totally unexpected and supportive response. I learned so many other people had been traveling the same path I had, and it ended up with all of us in that room.

SUPPORT CREW

Inside that drab building in Jersey, many people reached out to me and thanked me for talking about my addiction and for opening up. They didn't know who to talk to, either, and had the same feelings of isolation as I did. It made me realize there are many people out there struggling with something in their lives. Whatever form it takes, those struggles often bring feelings of guilt or shame.

Shame, however, can be changed to courage by one simple yet scary act: opening up and being authentic. My fear of being judged was alleviated as I crawled out of my shell. As I stood there and shared my story, I fully expected to be judged, and instead, I experienced the opposite: people actually embraced me. I hardly knew how to respond. In that moment, I realized something monumental: at their core, people have good hearts and are empathetic to others. Yes, everyone has problems and challenges, and talking about those things can be very difficult. Still, even with this clarity, I still struggle with laying it all out there. I know there is a chance I will be judged, that my employees, for example, might learn of my deficiencies. In fact, at one point, some of my staff did hear more than a few details of my private life that I would have rather kept aside from work. However, with some of them, such a high level of transparency built loyalty between us, not ambiguity.

My experience has been that by opening up and sharing, you can manifest the same type of openness from others with the same or similar situations. This creates a community with a common bond and allows you to develop deeper relationships, regardless of the situation, with people who offer selfless support—something you'll likely need as you navigate your journey to obtaining fulfillment in your life.

THE POWER OF ACCOUNTABILITY

The best thing about a circle of friends with genuine concern is that they will hold you accountable and call you out on missteps. You *want* them to hold you accountable because it makes it tougher for you to make excuses or drift away from obligation.

Case in point: recently, I had a stretch where I hadn't been to a GA meeting for over a month for a litany of reasons. A couple of times, the meetings conflicted with volunteer work I planned. Other times, I was at the gym or just taking a break. One day, I received a text from a group member announcing an upcoming meeting they wanted me to attend. I was on my way to the gym, and without that text, I would not have considered the meeting. I had fallen out of my routine, and it's always tough to get back into it.

The text held me accountable, and I am glad it came. "Hey," the message said. "You've been a big part of the room. Where have you been? We're having a meeting this Monday. Your thoughts, your wisdom, and your recovery are needed." I thanked the sender, and it turned out to be a huge step to getting me back on track. I blocked out Mondays from then on to dedicate to these Gamblers Anonymous meetings. I needed that in my life because in the end, it aided my ongoing recovery tremendously. By listening to other people's struggles, it reminded me of how far I had come and that, now, I could talk to and help others.

ENABLERS IN MY PERSONAL LIFE

Enablers have surrounded me since my gambling and partying days in New York City. My life was a nonstop parade of negative reinforcement. At my level of addiction with gambling, natural selection steered me toward others of like mind. I would sit at a bar to watch game after game, gambling on them all, while others at the bar were doing the same thing. After talking about gambling the entire time, we'd inevitably end up in card games later that night, gambling again. We all shared the same habit, and soon, we were hanging out all the time. I started to believe these people were real friends.

While nearly all of my time was spent gambling, much of it was also spent in isolation and misery. Even surrounded by ten so-called friends at a table, hyped up on Fantasy Football, I simply felt alone. We would drink all day, do drugs, and dedicate our lives to creating negative energy. Because we enabled each other, this scenario didn't just continue but began to escalate. I knew it was a damaging environment, but at the time, I thought I loved it, and it was what I knew. I was also numbing all other emotions in my life. I was comfortable, and I was an addict, so I kept coming back and coming back and coming back.

There wasn't an escape or break from the gambling world with my so-called friends there. If I wanted to take a day off from gambling, without fail, the phone would ring, and someone would want to talk scores or spreads. Inevitably, we'd end up going somewhere to bet on horses, cards, sports—*something. Anything.* It was a vicious cycle. The disease took over. While at work, I would play Party Poker, an online poker game, betting big stakes and minimizing the window on my computer when the boss would walk by. When I went with friends to dinner, we would play credit card roulette to determine who would pay the bill. I was sick, and I admit it. All conversations focused on gambling, drinking, or partying. We hung out every day, and I didn't know a thing about most of them. We were strangers disguised as friends, held together through addiction.

The money allowed us to party like rock stars. We had such little respect for that money that it disgusts me to think about it today. We'd gamble all day and blow a bushel of cash at the club at night. At the time, I thought it was great fun, but it got me nowhere. In fact, it got worse. The addiction spiraled downward to drug use. I would be at the club with friends and a table full of women and leave to gamble alone online. This high wasn't enough for me. I would need something to get me to that next level, and for me that happened to be cocaine. I went through cycle after cycle of snorting coke, gambling online, smoking weed, and popping pills to eventually get some sleep. It was disgusting, out-of-control behavior as I look back upon it, but nobody knew about it. I kept it hidden and turned into a zombie—wouldn't answer my phone, wouldn't leave the house. I was high all day, gambling, eating, and gambling some more. This period of my life is one of deep shame. I was a completely useless human being, driving myself away from anyone important to me.

ENABLERS IN MY PROFESSIONAL LIFE

Enablers don't just surround addicts; they can surround business people too.

Eventually, I got some semblance of an act together and snapped out of my destructive lifestyle. Now in Salt Lake City, Utah, with a successful business growing and several years removed from gambling, I had money I wanted to invest. I frequented a bar in Salt Lake City to watch football and hang out. One day, I learned a couple of the regulars were opening a new club across the street. They were looking for investors, so I asked them to shoot me a proposal.

Although I didn't know much about the people, their proposal looked solid to me, and the thought of being a part owner in a bar seemed awesome. I would be "big man on campus," and that was damn appealing and something my ego always chased. I looked it over and agreed to invest $60,000 of my own money into the bar/club—a good move on the surface, as it turned out to be the hottest place in the city for the first year. I lived in a great condo across the street from the bar and partied there all the time. I was exactly what I wanted to be—"big man on campus," selecting people from the line outside to bring in directly for VIP treatment. My phone rang constantly with people looking to hang out. I got to know a new crowd, all from the club scene. Although it was a total distraction from my business connections, I had a blast. I did favors for my new so-called friends because I could. The whole scene was about money and power. Again, I convinced myself these were *my* people because I didn't know any better.

Until they weren't.

Two of the main people I invested with, who were partners in the bar, were stealing all the cash from the business from under our nose. Turns out one of them had a drug problem and the other was hooked on gambling. Although no laughing matter, I had to laugh at myself at the irony of the situation. After everything I had lived, there I was, being screwed by a gambler. And I found out the hard way.

When the bar scene dried up, my "people" all of a sudden disappeared.

I had no idea these business partners were siphoning off

my investment. My role was as an investor, and I focused on marketing the bar and bringing in customers. I wasn't involved day to day or on the operation side. A little over a year after the bar was open, I got an urgent call from one of the waitstaff. She indicated I needed to get to the bar right away because the police were there to shut down the establishment. Later, I learned my "partners" owed a huge chunk of money and weren't paying their taxes or paying the rent. So besides being out of business, all the paychecks to the staff were delayed, which I found out was a consistent pattern. The situation was complete chaos. Luckily, though, I didn't lose my entire investment. I negotiated with one of the partner's fathers (whose name was also on our contract) and worked out a fifty-cents-on-the-dollar return. At that point, I didn't think I would recover anything, so I was somewhat content losing only $30,000. Still, I felt outright betrayed, stabbed in the back, and helpless to do anything about it.

In the end, although I worked hard for my money, I simply didn't respect it and failed to see what was happening around me. I did not choose wisely. I partnered with people I thought were my friends and whom I believed I could trust, but in reality, they did nothing to earn that trust at all. I did not vet them properly, and I paid for it. I lost.

FEELING ALONE IN A FULL ROOM

If there was a road paved with bad luck and poor decisions, I seemed to always be on it and would continue to manifest it. As I look back, I attribute a lot of this to my negative doomsday mindset. This continued after I bought out my business partner when I wanted to expand the business and add an office in New York City. My plan was to hire three senior people, all with different staffing backgrounds, and jumpstart the New York operation with a credit line. I thought if I had senior-experienced leaders from different backgrounds within the recruiting industry, we would all be able to collaborate and make the best decisions for the company.

Unfortunately, it didn't turn out that way. My trio of amazing senior leaders didn't get along at all, and I did a terrible job handling the conflict. They complained about each other to me and complained about me to each other, and I just didn't want to deal with it. I hired a salesperson who became close with my director of recruiting, and they would Skype messages back and forth all day. Because I was often in the same room, I knew something was going on between them but couldn't put my finger on it. I tried to stealthily unearth the truth but only ended up micromanaging the whole thing. I simply couldn't let it go. I was not focusing on the business but creating more drama by micromanaging the entire situation.

I thought, *I am paying them a shit ton of money, and here they are messaging each other all day*. I believed they were trying to screw me over, and I was not going to tolerate it. I was so tied to the money invested in them that I looked at this as a betrayal. I felt like I needed to know what was going on and be a part of all its inner workings.

My micromanagement made the situation worse and created tension. Eventually, the sales associate wasn't performing the way I needed him to. I learned many of his Skype messages mentioned negative things about me, discussed skipping out on work, and alluded to various romantic dalliances. The messages revealed he smoked pot at work and snuck out to go to movies. I confronted him, and he lied about it all, so I fired him. But I didn't do it quietly. Instead, I delivered a rant about him cheating me, the company, and himself. I printed all of the Skype messages out and threw them down in front of him, calling him out on his bullshit in a public restaurant. His friend who he had become very close with—my director—heard about the whole thing, so I had the same confrontation with her. I handled both firings in an unprofessional and immature way because I was overly emotional about the situation and how much it was costing me in lost productivity. Again, it was always about the money. With my short-term thinking, I always took it personally because I deemed this behavior as betrayal. Looking back, I realize my behavior was not appropriate for someone trying to run a successful business. At the time, though, I simply couldn't see it, so I self-sabotaged a lot, driven by my emotional state.

I felt the same kind of all-consuming frustration outside of work, too, like I was being screwed over again and nobody understood. My attitude was shit almost every day. I didn't have anyone to talk to at the time, and I had no idea how to handle negative situations. Instead of trying to understand and build relationships, I was volatile. A walking time bomb. I had created my own chaos trying to manage three different offices without adequate staff, and I was stretched to the breaking point with one company or client responsibility after another near-constant crises.

Still embroiled in a lawsuit at the time and in my manic state, I got into screaming matches with my lawyer, arguments with staff, and disagreements with clients. I had a senior vice president drawing a large salary, and we verbally brawled constantly. I brought in an executive coach, but that didn't seem useful at all. It appeared the coach simply agreed with everything I said to keep being paid. (At least this was my assessment.) The issues at the office remained. I ditched the coach and bought my senior vice president out of his contract, which cost me $50,000. I had agreed to a terrible contract in the first place and was now paying for it. I felt like I should have his loyalty and agreement simply because I was paying him. When I *didn't* have his loyalty, I figured, he must be against me. Again, I equated everything with money and more betrayal.

I felt like the world was conspiring against me. The staff was out to get me. The bank was out to get me. I withdrew and cocooned into a place of isolation and self-pity. It felt like a twelve-round fight, and I was consistently being knocked down. I could never calm down during the heat of the days, and I literally smoked myself to sleep nightly.

But even in all the darkness and stress, I vowed to get back up and fight until I found a way forward. I took a hard look at reality, put my tail between my legs, shut down the New York office, and went back to Salt Lake City. I had to start somewhere, and New York was a source of significant financial and emotional stress, so I left, and this time for good.

WHAT IT ALL MEANS TO YOU: THE CURSE OF THE BUSINESS LEADER

When you're in the thick of it, running a company or starting one from scratch, it can feel like nobody relates. You can feel like you're on an island all by yourself. We sometimes have delusions of grandeur and may have a laser focus on building our companies to be the biggest and best. I think it is common for many business leaders, however, to feel a fair amount of isolation that comes with so much responsibility.

Many times, in the heat of establishing and growing a company, we are not ready for the demands involved. We think we can do it all and put far too much pressure on ourselves. It can be easy to throw yourself so far into the business that you withdraw from everything and everyone else in your life. When things go bad or stress hits a high note, you often have no one there to talk to and no plan to fall back on.

We all need support systems, but we must start with internal strength. I've learned it's vital to have a strong inner foundation to make rational—not emotional—decisions. Unfortunately, I mostly made the latter, and much of that impulse grew from feeding my ego and my desire for more money. I remember my insatiable desire to get back to New York City and build my business—to make it *bigger*. To make *more*. In the end, I wanted to show everyone how successful I was, and I didn't care about anything else. I had nothing in place to give me fulfillment and perspective. I stopped working out, had a habit with pills, and spent weekends getting stoned. Aside from sporadic volunteer work, I didn't do anything positive for myself. It all fed into negative behaviors.

In 2013, my world began to turn for the better, and once

again, it all started with surrounding myself with positive people. My company made the *Inc. 5000 List*, celebrating the 5,000 fastest growing companies in the country—a list we made for three consecutive years. I was proud of that and attended a gala event in Maryland. After the event, I joined a buddy at a bar and met a few people from the Young Entrepreneur Council (YEC), an invite-only group of like-minded entrepreneurs. I didn't know anything about these types of organizations at the time because I didn't allow myself to. I was too wrapped up in my own world of work and drama to look for positivity and fellowship around me.

The founders of YEC told me about their organization and invited me to an event the next night. There were scores of dynamic entrepreneurs with riveting stories of what they were trying to build, and I found them inspiring. That night, I engaged in several great conversations, and the experience drew me in so much that I joined the organization. For the first year, I didn't participate in any of their events or programs that they offered. Then, I truly started embracing it, and the timing couldn't have been better.

The next year, I attended an annual YEC event in Eden, Utah, called YEC Escape—a four-day entrepreneur gathering with skiing, fireside chats, and high-level engagement. I, along with about fifty other entrepreneurs, spent the time in the mountains participating in all manner of outdoor activities and making connections. The outdoor events coupled with the fireside chats, private cabins, amazing meals, and other perks put me in an amazing atmosphere with positive, like-minded individuals who I could build strong bonds and relationships with.

The second and third years in the program, I started to open up, reach out to people, and build strong and rewarding friendships. I attended similar events and got more involved. I didn't notice it at the time, but I started to evolve out of my isolation. Why? I had a solid five to ten trusted entrepreneurs I could call on to talk about challenges I would face running the business as well as personal challenges I was experiencing. We could share similar situations and offer one another guidance. It was a support system—both professionally and personally—that I hadn't had before, and it was a big step in getting me on the right track.

LESSONS LEARNED

Whether it was random luck or fate that I ran into the people from YEC, the lesson is that I *acted* on the opportunity without second-guessing or overthinking it. YEC isn't the only option out there for entrepreneurs either. There are dozens of supportive organizations within easy reach that offer a solid infrastructure and access to connect with uplifting and positive people. There are also other organizations that are not specifically entrepreneurially driven that focus on collaboration and support on specific areas of interest. A little research will go a long way, but it all starts with taking action.

If you happen to be a product manager, for example, there are groups dedicated specifically to the product management world. Same with a software engineer, a financial advisor, or a CTO. You can investigate various groups and programs that support your passion and join. It only takes that first step. Until you take it, nothing will change. I've discovered part of the challenge of overcoming isolation, anger, and fear is all about training your brain (or, in my case, retraining it) to take care of yourself and put yourself in a position of positivity, both seeking and offering guidance when the time is right.

When you recognize you're in a time of isolation or weakness, it can be a sign of your strength. If you see areas where you can improve or would like to increase your knowledge, *that's* the strength that guides you to becoming a better person, a business leader, spouse, friend, etc. If you set that mindset and let it lead the way, you can put yourself on the path to fulfillment, joy, and success.

CHAPTER SIX

FINDING FLOW

Finding flow is a stage in your journey where you shift into limitless thinking and living that builds on the new confidence and optimism that come from having a support network. It leverages that to a more radical shift in mindset—one where you learn to clear out limiting beliefs and follow your intuition, which allows you to live in a more effortless manner. But what does that mean, exactly?

"Going with the flow" sounds easy enough, right? There's more to it than that. Personally, with ample helpings of drama, addiction, and emotional stress, I had a tough time rolling with situations. Adversity is a strange animal, however, and it eventually allowed my vision to clear. Finding a flow to my life started with a commitment to always follow my intuition. Looking back at significant life events, I thought I was following my intuition; however, during those times, I was actually following money. My mind distorted what my intuition was telling me that led me to act this way for years. I didn't have a baseline of core, flow-enhancing beliefs that aligned with who I really am. Attending my first YEC event was the first time intuition clicked with my internal person.

Clearing old limiting beliefs and emotional wounds lays the groundwork for flow, allowing you to step further into following your intuition, which we all have access to. It allows you to manifest more optimal futures. Flow is living in a state of mind where exponential success and growth happen in your life and business effortlessly. It's about following your heart and intuition to how you live your life. There's no overthinking. No second-guessing. In a state of flow, if a decision is not a "Hell yes," it should be a "F— no." There is no in between.

Finding flow is difficult for many people to do because most of us make decisions with our heads, not our hearts and intuition. We put everything going on in our lives— family, friends, obligations, money—on the table in a neat, orderly fashion instead of throwing caution to the wind and trusting that our heart will lead us to the right place. Flow is more than just going with your gut, though. The methodology behind the practice is first clearing out negative, limiting beliefs and old emotional wounds. Once you create that baseline of flow and settle into it, it allows you to effortlessly accelerate the speed at which you can take a vision or an idea and make it reality. Sounds simple, right?

Look at this a bit closer. The basic premise of flow is not allowing limiting beliefs to control your actions. If you have a fear of heights, for example, that limiting belief will become an action (or inaction) and will prevent you from sightseeing at the top of the largest building in a city, going skydiving, or possibly even flying. If you're not a fan of the water, your limiting beliefs will hold you back from pursuing a desire to swim, jet ski, or go scuba diving. It may eliminate that desire altogether. Shying away from relationships because you have a limiting belief surrounding your potential for heartbreak takes you off the path of finding your perfect partner. Releasing those limiting beliefs, however, can open a world you might not have thought was possible.

TRANSFORMATION, BALI-STYLE

My road to finding flow traveled through Bali, Indonesia. Bali had been on my bucket list for years, and I spotted a Facebook post on the YEC's group wall for an opportunity to visit Bali. There was a retreat being held in Bali called "Unconventional Life." I didn't know what this event was even about, and I didn't bother investigating it before giving the opportunity a "Hell yes." I simply saw the post that day and reacted immediately and applied.

After I expressed strong interest, I had an interview with the head of Unconventional Life, Jules Schroeder. She told me they were looking for people with energy like mine who had been looking to live their life on their terms and may have faced challenges in doing so in the past. After describing parts of my personal journey and that I had just raised $75,000 for the Leukemia & Lymphoma Society, I was approved on the spot and went home to start planning. Still, I didn't know details of the program or the extent of the trip, and I didn't care. I was going to Bali, baby!

Because of the travel required and the geography of my business, I visited my India team for a week before heading to Bali. Unconventional Life provided comfortable accommodations at a villa on the mainland. I knew some of the attendees from prior events and conversations, and I met the remaining twenty or so participants in the first two days. The conference was made up of the traditional fare: breakout sessions, speakers, video presentations and—most of all—connection. They offered sessions on writing business plans, building and examining relationships, sponsoring your own retreat—things of that nature.

The session that stood out to me the most, though, focused on flow. A man and a woman, whom I later came to know as Jackie Knechtel and Justin Faerman, walked to the front of the room and took the floor. They began talking about how their lives changed when they started living in flow. They presented examples I found difficult to believe, but I listened nonetheless.

They both had successful careers. Jackie ran a six-figure private autism practice, where she made great money and had a huge impact on people's lives. She went sailing in the Hamptons on her days off and bought her first apartment at twenty-six years old. Justin had a dream job where he built and ran a multimillion-dollar division at one of the world's top green technology companies. He set his own hours, surfed with the CEO regularly, and had a revenue share deal on the growing profits of the company.

However, inwardly, Jackie felt empty and was always trying to prove herself. As a people pleaser and an overachiever, she worked insane hours and constantly felt stressed and burnt out. She was a control freak who micromanaged every part of her life.

Justin, despite the outward-looking success, felt trapped like a bird in a golden cage. Every day at the company, he felt like his soul was dying. He yearned to have the freedom to create his own life but struggled with letting go of the fear and uncertainty if he left. So they both went on a journey to discover why their lives were good but not great. They went deep within their own hearts and minds and also worked closely with the world's top coaches, healers, and spiritual teachers. Through that work, they stumbled into "the flow."

Ultimately, Jackie and Justin both left their day jobs to travel the world, and they started spending their time doing what they most wanted to be doing. Jackie was contracting to work with the children of a high-profile Saudi family and was offered $10 million to open her own autism clinic. Justin left his high-paying corporate job to hang out on the beach and spend time surfing while he watched his recently launched magazine and coaching practice thrive. They saw exponential growth and success happen effortlessly by living deeply in the flow. After experiencing this, they spent years doing field research into the mechanics and mindset shifts that allow people to live deeply and effortlessly in flow. They found that there were specific powerful shifts that needed to be made and specific inner blocks that needed to be cleared. They discovered that once those fell into place, everything clicked, and flow would happen spontaneously.

I sat in the crowd with thirty or so other people, and I was feeling very skeptical. I remember turning to the person next to me as they gave examples and saying, "She's giving all these examples of living in flow and how this was all meant to be. This sounds like a bunch of bullshit." I thought it was all part of them trying to sell us something. I was not open to listening to people talk about flow, energy, astrology, or anything of the sort. I thought this was all a joke and never would take these people seriously or even listen to them. Looking back, I realize this was all due to my complete ignorance of what flow actually was. Initially, it all felt like a scam. Even in Bali, a small part of me was still worried about getting taken, brainwashed, or screwed.

A fellow entrepreneur, who was enduring my bitching, turned to me then. "Just chill. Listen to what they have to say," she said.

I mumbled expletives and reluctantly agreed as I sat there in my negative haze. A few minutes later, something unexpected happened. The speakers started taking questions, and at the end, I literally felt an energy take over my body and raise my hand, although I had no conscious intention to actually raise it. It was an unintentional reaction, but I let it happen. Then, on that island among thirty new people (of which I knew only two or three of them), I opened up in front of the group. I spilled all the details of my addiction, isolation, drug use, lawsuit, company, and other bad karma that left me in that miserable state of mind.

I felt supported as I told my story, and the organizers asked me to stay and talk after their presentation was through. They said they'd helped people in similar situations find flow. *Yeah, whatever. I've heard that before*, I thought. Still, I agreed to meet with them—again, it seemed, by a choice not altogether my own.

After the presentation ended and we left the room, ten different people in the audience came up to me and hugged me. This completely caught me off guard. They offered comments like, "That was really brave," and "Thanks so much for sharing." Some attendees shared their own addiction issues with me privately. Afterward, the head of the entire retreat, Jules Schroeder, invited me for a short walk just to be sure I was okay. In spite of feeling a bit awkward, it felt good to spend some quiet time with her and share things I typically kept hidden.

The day before I left Bali, Jackie and Justin pulled me aside and asked to talk. As we chatted for well over an hour, I went through my entire story again, including how the stress of my never-ending lawsuit was affecting me. It was an incredibly open conversation, and they assured me they could help. "Look," Jackie said, "you can react to this any way you choose. You are in control of your emotions and can either embrace the situation or fight it."

The pair offered an online course on flow and recommended I take it as a tool to help me live a more effortless, enjoyable life. The course cost a little more than $1,000. Prior to the retreat, all my decisions were money-based, and my natural, initial reaction was one of resistance to a $1,000-plus price tag, especially because I thought the course might be a scam. However, on the flight back to the US, I thought it over. I thought to myself, *Would it be so bad to live a different way?* It felt really light—the exact opposite of the heavy feeling I always carried with me, as if I were allowing the legal matters and everything I was dealing with to weigh me down like a one-hundred-pound weight pressing against my chest. That light feeling felt good and optimistic. Living life in a positive state of mind? Appreciating that there is a positive lesson to be learned in even, what I deemed, the worst of situations? Was this possible? When I sat with the thoughts of this freeing feeling, it sounded so much better than being completely pissed off and miserable every time something bad happened. So I decided to follow my heart. I signed up for the course—a decision that would allow me to discover living in flow, would affect the perspective I held, and would completely change my decision-making process.

The course itself was involved, but as I embraced the process, many crazy, positive things began happening in my life. For example, I was scheduled to go to the South by Southwest Festival (SXSW), the annual tech, music, and film festival held in Austin, Texas. I had booked my flight in advance, but I didn't have a place to stay. In the past, I would always have to have my plans booked well in advance—my flight, car, hotel, passes to the conference, dinner reservations, and industry party lists. Whatever could be scheduled was, as I put tremendous pressure and stress on myself to ensure all angles were covered.

While I was taking the course on flow, though, I was clearing limiting beliefs and practicing living in flow—a practice that includes allowing life to flow effortlessly. So after finding out all the hotels were basically booked up well in advance, I decided not to worry about where I was going to stay and trust that it would work out. I didn't even think about it until two days before the event. I decided to give my friend Zeke a call. He lives in Austin, and I wanted to see if he had any friends who had an Airbnb I could rent.

"Zeke, hey, it's Dash," I said. "I am scheduled to head down to South by Southwest, and I don't have a place to stay yet. I was curious if you had any friends that might be renting out their place."

He paused. Silence.

"Man, you have some unbelievable timing! I just decided last night that I am taking my entire family to Hawaii, starting tomorrow, for the whole festival. You can stay in my 3,500-square-foot place for free. All I ask you to do is to feed our gerbil while I am away."

I couldn't believe my good fortune. He continued.

"That's not all, bro," he said. "You can also use my brand-new Mercedes truck the entire time."

I loved this feeling. How could this get any better?

"Oh, and I forgot to tell you that I will give you a parking pass to use my company's parking garage right on the main street where the festival is happening."

I couldn't believe it! When I was reporting these events back to the flow group, they told me this was not just good fortune or luck, but instead, it was truly what is meant by living in a state of flow. It was effortless, and the setup was killer. I was so stoked, and it gave me fuel to dive deeper into the flow.

This example resonated with me in a big way. I had tried so hard to find a solution for my dilemma of no place to stay. Hotel rooms were booked, and what was available was not reasonably affordable. As I started aligning myself with flow, I actually manifested a solution. And not just any solution but a damn good solution. Both the business accelerator in Bali and the online course deeply hinged on the premise that things happen at the right time for the right reason, and it's no coincidence. It is the universe conspiring with you. Once I internalized that belief, that vibe continued to play its hand in more significant areas in my life.

FLOW PRINCIPLE #3
FOLLOW YOUR INTUITION AT ALL TIMES

"All great achievements ... must start from intuitive knowledge. I believe in intuition and inspiration ... At times I feel certain I am right while not knowing the reason."

- **Albert Einstein**

Intuition is a funny thing. It doesn't always make sense, but it's always right. If you ask a spiritual teacher they'll tell you its a message from your soul and if you ask a scientist they'll tell you it has something to do with the quantum field. Personally we believe it's kind of like Switzerland—somewhere in the middle— a mixture of both the known and the yet to be known.

But regardless of what we or anyone believes for that matter, learning to tune into and heed your intuition is one of the most powerful things you can do to calibrate your life to the flow. That's because your intuition dynamically adjusts itself to the ever changing circumstances and conditions that exist whenever you need to make a decision.

It takes into account a huge number of variables that your conscious mind cannot even begin to comprehend, let alone process, and guides you (as effortlessly as possible, of course) towards the choices that will provide the most beneficial outcome for you and everyone involved.

Imagine for a second that you are playing a game of chess against a powerful supercomputer. How many moves in advance can you see before things get hazy? Maybe two or three at most until the number of possible combinations of moves and countermoves you and the computer could make becomes so complex it is beyond the capability of your conscious mind to keep track of, let alone make sense of.

Now consider the supercomputer you are playing against. In a few nanoseconds—instantaneously for all intents and purposes—it can foresee every possible combination of potential scenarios that could occur and make the ideal move given whatever circumstances are present at that very moment.

If you haven't guessed it already, the computer is a metaphor for your intuition—one of your greatest allies for getting you firmly into the flow.

But let's be clear here: intuition is a two way street—it's not always excitement and inspiration. Sometimes it's a gut wrenching 'hell no' to a job you're about to take or some other potentially life-changing decision where you've got some skin in the game.

Take Steve Jobs, for example. His intuition told him to drop out of college and study calligraphy. That was his highest excitement in that moment... and I'm sure his parents were simply thrilled with his decision. But Steve marched to the beat of a different drum and heeded his intuition—aligning himself with two of the core principles of flow—and where he ended up is the stuff of legends.

The principles always lead to your highest fulfillment and growth. *Always.*
Learn more at flow-mastery.com

The benefits of living in flow again showed themselves more recently. I was talking to Jules, who was scheduling the next Unconventional Life event. She called me up, as she did with all potential attendees, and told me that she was planning on having an epic event with seventy-five attendees this time—up from the twenty-five or thirty people who were in Bali. She was considering several places and mentioned Jamaica and Nicaragua as two of the options. It looked like more people wanted to go to Jamaica, she reported. In my opinion, though, Jamaica didn't excite me, especially since the event I went to was in one of the most majestic places in the world, Bali.

But Nicaragua? Now that seemed very intriguing. *When in the world would I ever have an opportunity to go to Nicaragua?* I thought. How cool would that be! I wasn't going to go to Jamaica if she held it there. I simply told her that, in my opinion, Nicaragua felt much more aligned with the soul of what her event was. She said she would think about it, but it looked like Jamaica was coming together based on the people in each country with whom she was working to secure the location. After I hung up, I thought to myself that as much as I wanted to be back with the amazing souls that I had met in Bali, there was just something about Jamaica that wasn't sitting with me. Several weeks passed, and the announcement came: Nicaragua was the location! In a state of flow, I signed up immediately and believed I manifested it through that very conversation.

When I spoke to Jules a few weeks later, I asked her what happened and why she changed countries. She said that it was something in the conversation that we had that pulled her to seeing if Nicaragua would be possible. Before our conversation, she was having difficulty identifying a location that could fit up to seventy-five people. Jules explained to me that after our call, "everything for Nicaragua just started falling into place. All the effort that I was putting in to finding an event space before was leading me to dead ends. They just didn't have anything big enough. After we spoke, though, everything started flowing."

While at the event in December 2017, I was on stage giving a lightning talk. Jules came over and explained that very story to all seventy-five attendees. This is another small example I credit to living in flow. If I didn't experience it firsthand, I wouldn't believe it myself. In the past, I would judge what you just read and probably roll my eyes, but that was the old way of thinking that I've happily left behind.

I continued to embrace this new mindset by manifesting my future and following my intuition. By openly speaking about the goals I wanted to achieve and what I wanted to do, I was manifesting things into my life that were working themselves out for my benefit. Life was finally conspiring for me. I chose to take deep breaths instead of stressing about situations I couldn't control. Time and time again, solutions appeared at the right time and for the right reason.

FREE FROM THE CONSTRAINTS OF MONEY

The idea of not having a giant headache or feeling like a giant asshole all the time became very attractive after my Bali experience and after studying flow. My mindset shifted, and I relaxed. Previous to this, I was constantly thinking about the business and the lawsuit. In fact, I couldn't stop thinking about it all day and all night. *What if I lost the lawsuit? What if I lost it all?* I only had doomsday thoughts. But now I had a new mindset. *Big deal if I lost the suit and the company*, I now thought. If I really ended up losing the business, I was fully confident that I'd figure it out. I'd get by. I could move to any tropical island and sell more coconuts than anyone else on the island. I was a natural salesman, after all, and I realized the financial melee was not the end-all-be-all in my life. Suddenly, I had clarity: whatever happened, happened, and I could either let it control my emotional state throughout my life or define my own life and my own happiness. I chose the latter and will every single time for the rest of existence.

I have since moved into a completely different state of mind: happiness, or fulfillment, is now defined by living life to the fullest, seeking meaningful relationships and experiences, having empathy and helping others, scheduling fun well ahead of time, and stepping into the person I know I can be.

If you are a business leader or family breadwinner, I understand what it feels like when you have a certain image to uphold. People think of you and respect you in a different way if you are a successful professional or deemed a success at all. I know because I've been there. People often tell me that because I've had a business for eleven years, I am a success story and an inspiration, but I feel the opposite. I had been living in a world of negativity and hid it from everyone, creating a shield between my family, my employees, my friends, and most importantly, myself. I never had shared emotionally how entrepreneurship—and how being so tethered to money in such a negative way—really felt. One thing I knew for sure was that money was not the answer to any sort of fulfillment I was seeking.

CHANGES ON THE HOME FRONT

Ironically, my changes at home started on an island halfway around the world in Bali. The first day I was there, I met Raya, who was helping run the Bali Unconventional Life Retreat and who also happened to be Jules's younger sister. The first conversation we had was incredibly deep—deeper than I normally would go with anyone, especially someone I'd just met. I don't remember how or why it came up, but I told her, "I am so addicted to TV right now, and it's such a waste of my time. I end up isolating myself and watching hours of the worst reality television there is." I remarked that I'd love to just get rid of the TV and be free of the habit and the unhealthy hold it had on my life.

"Well, then just get rid of it," she replied.

It sounded like such a simple and obvious suggestion, but it resonated with me. Right then and there, I decided to get rid of my cable TV boxes.

"Okay, I'll do it. I'm going to get rid of it," I committed to her and put it in the calendar on my phone. It felt so good to say those words out loud, and I couldn't wait to get home and cut another addiction loose. Ironically, I had this conversation before the introduction of flow. In retrospect, I can see I created flow on my own before truly understanding what it was. At the time, I only knew I was driven by a desire to simplify my life and live opposite of my addictive personality and the chaos on which I thrived. It seemed so clear as I stood under Bali palm trees on a magical island and admitted how miserable TV made me. Surely, it would be easy to remove it from my life the minute I got home.

But it didn't happen like that.

I didn't get rid of cable the minute I got home like I'd intended. Instead, I intentionally watched the end of every terrible series that I had recorded on my DVR that I was addicted to. This process took about two weeks to get through. Perhaps subconsciously, I was weaning myself off yet another addiction. Still, I stuck with the plan. I woke up one morning and disconnected everything. I took those cable boxes and DVRs and drove to the Xfinity store location. I returned the boxes, snapped a picture of me at the store, and felt a huge weight lifted off my back. This may seem like a small thing to some, but it was a huge step for me. I had a spring in my step that day and wanted to continue that momentum.

I can attribute so much of my launch toward clarity to Bali. When I arrived on the island, I felt weighed down, like a big fish with hooks in it. One hook was obsession with reality TV. One hook was smoking pot every night. Another hook was the weight of managing three rental properties myself—worrying about keeping the tenants happy and constantly managing and fixing them. My business was a hook, as was the ever-increasing stress from my lawsuit. The loan to buy the business was a hook, and the Chase loan was another. I had so many hooks in my body that there was no way I could keep from getting snagged day after day.

However, when I got home from Bali and returned those cable boxes, I felt one of those hooks release. I felt lighter, so I wanted to share. I posted my big cable-dumping day on social media and received dozens of replies like, "That's the best decision you ever made. I got rid of mine three years ago." I had no idea I had so many supporters and like-minded people out there. I manifested the whole event to get free of that hook, and I glided into flow.

My next big step was to stop smoking pot every night. Pot was an escape for me. I often came home from work so stressed out and irritated that all I could do was get high so I didn't have to think about it. Along with smoking came unhealthy eating habits. I'm in fairly good shape, but I've never had the best eating habits. Still, I fancied myself as healthy overall.

Because we have a history of heart disease in our family, my mother urged me to visit a heart specialist. At my appointment, they found a partially blocked artery and diagnosed me with coronary heart disease. *What the hell?* I thought. *I run marathons. I'm healthy.* To combat the condition, the physician prescribed a diet that included drastically reducing fried foods and cheese, along with a host of other restrictions. For me, the biggest loss was having to give up fried foods. When I smoked pot, I'd eat bags and bags of potato chips with up to ten different dips. (I liked to keep it fun at least!) I was hooked on salty foods in general but now had to give up chips! Oh my God, what would I do? Exactly what I did do: give them up and find a better alternative.

I stepped up my game, though, and finally stopped smoking pot on a nightly basis. I always kept a stash of weed in the house, and I haven't even bought any in months. It feels good. As with any drug, I had challenges giving it up, and truth be told, I still occasionally dabble, but giving it up on a nightly basis was tough, especially when it came to my sleeping habits. When you smoke for so long, your body gets used to going to sleep a certain way, and I had to adapt to be able to sleep through the night. Now, though, my mind is clearer, and I feel better overall.

Turning away from pot was a significant hurdle for me because I convinced myself I'd never be able to stop smoking on a daily basis even though, in the back of my mind, I knew I could. Sounds familiar, right? Like the thought I could never stop gambling. All these years later, I still had the thoughts that I could not stop this addictive habit of mine. I had overcome the thought of never gambling again. Having been free of it for twelve years, I knew that with the proper support, I could accomplish anything. We all can. Addicts battle the desire to stop a drug with the fear of losing it. In my case, I thought I needed pot to deal with my stressed-out life. I did the back-and-forth dance for a long time, until one day it hit me: I was done with having it in my house. I wanted to be able to sleep without relying on any substance. I knew weed was holding me back, and the amount I was using was not serving any purpose in my life.

It's often not easy to quit anything you've relied on in your life, good or bad. I think any addict can attest to that. You don't just stop and forget all about it. You try to achieve insight and pursue a healthier way of living. You want to change things in your life, but you don't want to beat yourself up all the time while doing it. The goal is to open yourself up to learning about different ways to live and to make small changes that can have big results in your pursuit of a more fulfilled life. How? Start by testing and finding what sits with you best. For me, it was living in flow consciousness and following my intuition at all times. It's important to try new things, see how they fit in your life and personality, and settle on what gives you an overall sense of contentment.

Saying no to binge-watching TV, giving up my daily pot smoking, and not worrying so much about the what-ifs in life were all means to an end. I was searching for sim-plicity, a state the opposite of my usual tendency, which teetered on the verge of manic behavior. I was able to achieve this fulfillment in my life because I opened my mind and followed my intuition, and you can too.

ACCOUNTABILITY PARTNERS CREATE PROGRESS

On the last day of the Bali Unconventional Life Retreat, the group did an exercise where we sat in a circle and each asked for something we needed. If anyone else in the group could help, they connected and worked together. Some people were interested in business support, and others wanted to dive deeper into things like circling. Circling is a spiritual, interpersonal process that's equal parts art form, meditation, and group conversation that we participated in while there. Still others were offering a place to stay if anyone ever visited the home cities where they live. During this session, I mentioned I wanted to have accountability for my actions and would like to have "accountability partners" to help me stay on track. Two members of the group volunteered, and we set up regular calls to check in with each other and talk about our progress on projects, personal development, and goals we still wanted to accomplish in our personal and professional lives.

My accountability partner request was a fairly simple one, yet it helped keep me on a good path for a long period of time. It reaffirmed my belief that everyone can benefit from a coach, partner, or friend who can hold them accountable to things they are trying to achieve. It is easy to be pulled off course, and having someone to motivate you in reaching your goals can keep you on track.

I still struggle with keeping emotions in check and staying focused on being a good leader. The difference now is that I have the tools to recognize this quickly and correct the behavior. It is important to get past your insecurity, ego, or embarrassment and recognize the triggers that contribute to downward spirals or nonproductive behavior so you can course-correct, and that's where a mentor or coach can be extremely impactful. Everyone needs to bounce ideas off someone, share experiences and dreams, and stay accountable. If you're going to bet on something, bet on the value of being authentic and true to yourself.

LESSONS LEARNED

Even if you don't have the baggage I have in my life, embracing flow, positivity, and accountability can still help you find fulfillment in yours. My suggestions come from many experiences in a life rife with stressors, but they apply to a broad range of life situations. Don't shut doors before they are ever opened because of a perception you have. This was the exact behavior I consistently participated in. If your life isn't going the way you want it to and you feel trapped and in a place of negativity, misery, or isolation, you have the ability to change your situation. It doesn't matter how difficult or complicated you have convinced yourself it would be. Change is *easy*. It might take time, but it is easy. However, if you do not hold yourself accountable and put in the work, then nothing will change.

If you find yourself struggling, consider stepping back and trying to keep your ego in check. We operate much of our lives through our egos, and they constantly get in the way. Many times, we are afraid of how people judge us, so we judge them on how they're judging us. It can be a vicious cycle that others can drag you into if you let them. Most of the time, it's all perception, and it's in your head. We tell ourselves whatever story sounds best—whatever has the least amount of change or effort we will have to make. At the end of the day, the negative voices in our head are ours, and they don't matter. They create fear, which is directly tied to ego, and they often prevent us from being genuine to ourselves and those around us—a roadblock on the way to positive change.

Part of manifesting positive change is being open to new ways of thinking. Act. Say yes if it's a "Hell yes," and no if it's not. If you have a positive attitude, throw caution to the wind, throw cynicism out the door, and embrace this new way of making decisions. Then, magical things will happen. Resist your natural tendency to question what feels new or different. I firmly believe that letting go of limiting beliefs, following your intuition, and embracing a flow mindset allows you to literally change external reality to match that new mentality. It worked for me, and it can work for you too.

CHAPTER SEVEN

CHANGING YOUR REALITY

For me, changing reality was about becoming curious, learning new ways to approach situations, and incorporating new insights. Understanding that slipups happen, examining my unhealthy relationship with money, seeking out accountability partners, and following my highest intuition as much as possible when making daily life decisions (both small and big) has allowed me to shift into a much more positive reality. It's not always easy. Many people are afflicted with what I call "decision fatigue": an exciting opportunity presents itself, and their initial reaction is they are excited and want to do it. Then they start contemplating all the reasons they *shouldn't*: *I can't be out of work during that time. My family needs me to be home. I have a birthday party I need to go to. Contractors are scheduled to be at the house. It's too expensive for me to go...* and on and on. A consistent process of overthinking takes control, and the excitement initially felt through intuition fades. As you continue to kick the can down the road, the decision is never made, and the opportunity is missed.

Instead of dealing with a cycle of decision fatigue, try this: if it feels right, consider following those initial feelings and taking action that will allow you to control your reality. All the excuses we give ourselves have solutions. Making changes to your routines or surroundings to open yourself up to a new way of living won't always look the same way. Sometimes, you'll have an immediate, reactive decision when an amazing opportunity is put in front of you, and your intuition will take over. Other times, your change will be more proactive when you have a chance to act on something you manifested.

For me, a month-long trip to California was a bit of both. When writing this book, I decided I wanted to head out to the Los Angeles area and spend time on the ocean. A friend checked on rental homes and found two: a smaller home right on the water and a larger one a few blocks away. My original intention was to be on the ocean waterfront, but I started thinking it would be fun to have a larger place and invite friends out to visit. That was, after all, the main reason I wanted to go in the first place. The ocean has a certain calmness and roar at the same time that really touches my soul. After being told the beach house might not be available and I could act on the other location, I ultimately decided it was ocean or nothing. Sure enough, a couple of weeks later, the landlord made adjustments so I could spend a month in the house on the ocean before the new tenant moved in. Even in this example, I had some decision fatigue debating between these two locations. But in the end, I followed my original intuition, which was to be as close to the ocean as possible and manifested the ocean view. I could look out the window with the ocean a stone's throw away. I followed my intuition, manifested the opportunity, and acted on it.

The same thing happened in my business life. Besides Utah, where my home base is, I have clients in New York, Connecticut, Portland, and Miami. In the past, being a small business owner, I would always overthink making the long trips to visit them, worried about leaving the office, falling behind, and risking my employees slacking off if I wasn't there. I replayed these scenarios in my head repeatedly, even though I knew they had a very small chance of actually happening. Recently, though, I switched it up, making the decision to visit each location. I let go of those what-if scenarios and went on several visits to clients across the country. I had phenomenal trips, scored new business, and had time to explore places I had never seen. And yes, to be fair, some things did happen while I was away from the office, but they could have easily occurred if I stayed. I learned to let go of the things that I cannot control. I credit the serenity prayer in Gamblers Anonymous and other recovery programs for helping me achieve this. The prayer of, "God, grant me the serenity to accept the things I cannot change, courage to change the things I can, and the wisdom to know the difference," is one I heavily lean on. It has helped me in various aspects of life.

This new thought process allows me to control my own reality: if it feels right, I'm going to do it. I knew it felt right for me to go to LA and stay a month. If shit hit the fan back at the office, I knew I could simply fly back and handle it. I kept faith that everything would work out, and by adopting this mentality, I've also recognized opportunities in my life I hadn't seen before.

I continue to control my reality today. One day a friend from the Leukemia & Lymphoma Society reached out and asked if I'd like to join a fundraising trip to Africa to climb Mount Kilimanjaro. Once I heard, it just felt right, and I didn't even hesitate. It was a "Hell yes" decision for me. My brother had done the climb years prior, and it was something in the back of my mind. I followed my intuition and, along the way, learned that the company who would be guiding us on the climb also offered African safaris, a dream of mine since I was a small child. One of the trips happened to be departing right after the Kilimanjaro climb, so I said yes and signed up for a five-day safari immediately following the eight-day climb. The cover of this book is an actual photo looking out from the top of Mount Kilimanjaro.

Saying yes to the unknown can be scary, but it allows one to face their fears, live in flow, and experience life in a more free-flowing manner. It personally allowed me to let go of my control-freak behaviors and have more fulfillment in all areas of my life.

COMMITTING TO AUTHENTICITY

Another practice that helps me control my reality is my commitment to genuine authenticity, which is one reason I am revealing my struggles and weaknesses to the world. In the past, a lot of people *thought* I appeared as authentic when, in reality, I hid a great deal of stress, fear, anger, embarrassment, and frustration underneath the surface. Being truly authentic means opening yourself up and discussing or doing things that might make you uncomfortable without worrying about people's perceptions of you. Their perception of you is actually a reflection on them.

Because discomfort is essentially built in, committing to real authenticity is not an easy task. It can feel unnatural, as you need to let your guard down and be vulnerable.

For example, one of my business coaches had challenged me to do a Facebook Live to discuss my relationship with money and how it has changed. My initial reaction was resistance and hesitation. I made some excuses as to why I couldn't do it, but because it is of the utmost importance that I am as authentic as possible, I acquiesced. Once I allowed myself to fully consider the opportunity, though, I quickly realized the benefits. Although Facebook isn't exactly a standing-room-only audience, the talks became highly important to me because they allowed me to speak from the heart and open up. I needed that release even if I didn't know it, and I received very positive responses from my listeners that ended in engaged conversations.

Prior to doing any Facebook Lives, I rarely spoke to anyone about my money, business, or personal challenges. That was not a healthy approach, especially because those issues were such significant pieces of my life. Instead of leaning on other people in similar positions who could provide guidance, insight, and support, I held it all in. The overwhelmingly positive responses to my talks reinforced my belief that authentic people will gravitate toward other authentic people. After all, it's generally a turn-off when a person tries to constantly present a glossy, over-filtered image of their perfect life. We all know the social media stories about how amazing life is 100 percent of the time, but it's just not realistic. Social media can build bonds, like it did for me, but only when used to help you be true to yourself and to others. That's how real relationships are built. Since I've incorporated genuine authenticity in my life, I've carried it offline and am able to do a much better job running my company, managing challenges in business and life, controlling negative emotions, and most importantly, realizing I have the ability to pave my future any way I choose.

PRIORITIZING SIMPLICITY

In order to direct your life to where you want it to be and live with authenticity, the critical step is a familiar one: take action. For me, finding flow is what helped me turn the corner. For others, it could be exposing yourself to more positivity, overcoming a fear by stepping out of your comfort zone, stepping away from negative influences in your life, or overcoming a challenge you are facing. If you're in an unhappy marriage or relationship or a job you no longer enjoy, for example, you might recognize you're miserable but then feel as though you are stuck and have no other option. Why? Because the fear of the unknown can be scary. To remain in this state is paralyzing. It can be completely uncomfortable and feel like starting everything over from square one. You might be afraid of what the other side might look like or that you will be judged. So instead of following your heart and what you truly feel, you choose to stay stagnant. I say "choose" here intentionally: *not* taking action is a choice that every one of us has, just like taking action is too.

Similarly, are you an entrepreneur or leader who has too much on your plate and who can't seem to overcome your inner conflicts or demons? Are you continually focused on the next project, the next dollar, or the next sale to distract you from your problems? If so, you can feel like whatever decisions you make will not matter and will not change anything. You believe that change is difficult, when the truth is that *change is easy*. It just takes a little bit of courage. Whether personally or professionally, not taking action *seems* easier, but it can ultimately leave you sinking deeper and deeper into an unhealthy situation.

I've found the most efficient way to disengage from negative situations of any type is to determine a goal, set a progression of tasks to help you reach it, and get an accountability partner for whom you also return the favor. Enlisting the help of others along the way has been critical to my success, and it could help you too. I've found a daily action plan is a highly efficient tool that works for many people, but the crux of finding fulfillment and prioritizing simplicity is not all about specific practices; instead, it's about bringing lessons back into your world. I call it aligning the internal and external.

Reaching alignment doesn't happen overnight, and you

have to continually work to maintain this state once you reach it. For example, I still have many objectives I want to accomplish, but I have yet to act on them. Internally, I know I want to do a podcast, but I have yet to organize the content and execute that goal. I also want to speak to others to share the lessons I have learned so others in need know there is another way. Although these are goals of mine, I haven't fully developed a roadmap to get me to that place. Some goals come while practicing living in flow. After coming back from the trip to Bali, for example, I knew I wanted to live as close to the ocean as possible for a month because it truly soothes my soul. I made that intention a reality. As the opportunity presented itself, I seized it.

To make my outstanding internal goals tangible, I take the journal approach. I've found writing down everything I want to accomplish—and noting the tasks required to get me to that place—is an efficient method to help keep me organized and on track. I am a list type of person, so I form my journal in list fashion. The journal approach helps create a schedule with a plan, which lends itself well to bolstering personal accountability. If I write it down and it's on my calendar, it will get done.

LESSONS LEARNED

If you're feeling stuck in any way, I'd encourage you to

grab a notepad right now and write down five goals you want to meet and how you plan to meet them. It sounds simple, but I've explained in this chapter how freeing simplicity can be. You can reach this state by creating circumstances and events in your life that counterbalance the negativity you're experiencing, and the positives—or the anticipation of the positives—can help drive you forward. Living in a world of optimism and positivity feels so much lighter than carrying around animosity and negativity. I would know because I did it most of my life. The more you step out of your comfort zone and say yes to new things, the easier it will be to create change and live the reality you want to live. One small act can have a huge impact.

CHAPTER EIGHT

THE HABIT OF HABIT-MAKING

A close relative to living in flow and changing your reality is habit—the positive kind. In its simplest form, a habit is a pattern of consistency. As I know all too well, changing negative habits can be a challenge in today's crazy world, but it certainly is possible. With so much noise around us, though, it can be easy to get off track, and once you get off track, it's much harder to get back on.

To stay on track and maintain consistency with healthy habits, you can start by surrounding yourself with positive people. You will end up acting like the people with whom you surround yourself. If they are inspiring, positive, and supportive, the conversations you have will be of that nature and will keep you in the right mental space.

It will lead to more positive situations. There is more to it than that, though, because positivity begins within you. You can't always go seek it elsewhere. Some things that help me include incorporating some simple meditation into my life as well as taking care of my body by regularly exercising. These two simple examples allow my mind to sustain positive momentum. I know if I can't be the best to myself and treat myself with care, then I won't find what I'm looking for when seeking support or positive energy from others.

When cultivating a proactive, focused mindset and fostering positivity in your life, you're more apt to be better prepared when unexpected challenges *do* hit, and remember, they *always* do and *always* will. In those situations where we face hurdles in life, whether with our families, friends, businesses, health, or any other host of challenges life throws our way, positive habits can be the difference between having the tools you need to pick yourself back up and finding yourself sinking deeper. I've written about fulfillment in the pages of this book, and it is important to note that positivity serves as a counterbalance to the roadblocks and challenges we all inevitably face at some point in our lives.

For example, when I quit gambling, gave up my cable, and navigated through various business challenges, I would find at times that it was very difficult to breathe positivity into my life through this series of small habit changes. A key culprit is self-sabotage, a shadowy affliction that can sneak up on you when you least expect it. Sometimes, it can be so subtle you don't notice your self-sabotage is derailing your journey to making positive habits.

For example, I recently caught up with an entrepreneur in the early stages of establishing a software engineering consulting firm. He has been telling me for the past six months that his goal was to have fifteen people working for him and that he would like my guidance. Because I believe in supporting my fellow entrepreneurs, love helping people, and know how important it is to have a coach, I told him I'd offer to mentor him in any way I could. To start, I asked for some case studies that the company could pitch to potential clients. When I didn't get them, I asked again. And again. Every time, he apologized and said something came up that prevented him from getting me the material. Although his real objective was to scale up the company, secure a solid employee base, and get more business, he was too blinded by short-term gains to see he was undermining his own progress. Instead of prioritizing his goal, he put it on the back burner to pursue quick wins. Although his goal was clearly defined, he didn't create the time nor the habits needed to get there. Only after he and I talked through the issue did he realize his tendency to hold himself back. "You're right," he said. "I never thought of it that way, but I'm doing this to myself."

This example of the entrepreneur who thinks he's doing right by his business but isn't shows how your mind can undermine you. It's happened to me time and time again, and I finally learned from it. You can avoid this trap, as I now have, by creating habits that stick, not ones that put pressure on you to complete. If you're consistent, you're likely to see progress unfold as you steadily approach your goal. For me, writing this book required me to dedicate several hours of my time each week specifically to the task. It was a habit I created and had to maintain in order to finish the project. With the habit now firmly in place and the book in your hands, I'm committing those weekly hours to another productive task, whether it's promoting the book, speaking at events, mentoring other entrepreneurs, or working on my nonprofit. Making habits has become a habit for me and has transformed into an enduring lifestyle—one that replaced my old way of living of simply chasing another high.

HABITS CAN CREATE FULFILLMENT

The habit of habit-making is unique in that it can pave the path to both balance and variety, two forces that can serve you equally. Forming habits while living in flow means you open the door for new experiences that can end up being highly inspirational, but getting there takes work. When I stopped gambling, for example, I didn't know how to spend all my extra time. So I took up running marathons and trained obsessively. I ran those four marathons in five years, and while that seemed healthy, it was an obsessive action—a new healthier addiction but still an addiction. After two back surgeries, I eventually stopped running and dove into fundraising and volunteering for LLS—another activity that, on the surface, is a positive one. After all, who can argue with raising money to help fight a deadly disease? It seemed legit on the surface, yet no matter how healthy or noble my actions were, my approach was still that of one in an addictive, manic state. In between that time, I threw myself into my business even deeper than ever before, consumed by the thought of expansion and trying to single-handedly run three offices. I worked myself into misery. Then, of course, was the six-year lawsuit constantly hanging over my head, and that became an obsession and an addiction as well.

It's always a challenge, but we can set ourselves up for success by building a plan of habit-making. I learned a hard lesson post-gambling because even though I stopped gambling, that time was filled with zero positivity. I allowed negativity in and attracted it. I can look back now and see much of this was my own doing: I hadn't formed positive habits. I didn't take the time to make or adhere to any type of plan, even though I've always known I perform much better with a schedule. If I had tried to organize my world just a fraction, I believe it would have substantially reduced my stress level and avoided much of the negativity.

Even something as simple as managing weekend activities unfolds so much better with an action plan. If Friday rolls around and I have nothing planned, I usually end up having a dud weekend, isolated and not in a positive mindset. If I at least plan to do a couple of things consistently on weekends—such as going to the farmer's market, hitting the gym, attending a sound bath, or getting together with friends—my days turn out much better. Such a small step makes a tremendous difference for me and leads to not just a busier weekend but a more fulfilled week.

The brightest side of positive habits is their endurance, which is the exact flip side of chasing a short-term high. Dialing into a routine that positively influences your life can afford opportunities you may have missed otherwise. When I consistently smoked pot, it was a short-term high. Running marathons was another short-term high. Doing massive fundraising in short periods of time was yet another short-term high. They all felt good for different reasons, but they didn't last. I had created habits that, in effect, pulled me backward and left me floundering in a negative state as soon as I wasn't participating in them. It was like crashing down like an addict would coming off their high.

Attitude—often a reflection of the type of habits you have in your life—affects everything from your personal relationships to how you perform as a leader. Attitude is a little thing that makes a huge difference. Naturally, wandering around eternally irritated and stressed out is unlikely to inspire employees, clients, or for that matter, friends or family. Don't get me wrong: employees might see you come in every day and work your ass off, and odds are, they respect that, but inspiration is another beast altogether. Building positive, fulfilling habits breeds a laser focus and mental stability, and can lead to success in all areas of your life, both in and out of the office.

KNOW YOURSELF. BE YOURSELF. LIVE FULFILLED.

A stellar fringe benefit of habit-making is allowing you to be proactive in your life and giving you the space to become who you want to be. In doing so, you will come to know yourself better than ever before. Making and following habits that align you with your core values will help you define what you want to achieve and offer you the clear path to get there.

Take weight loss, for example. If you want to lose weight, you need to change your diet and exercise, both of which require changes in your lifestyle. Ideally, you'll need to change what you eat and incorporate a schedule that includes time at the gym, walking, riding your bike, etc. Regardless of what you choose, there must be a consistent behavioral pattern for you to have success.

The business world offers another example. If you're an entrepreneur or leader facing challenging times, you might struggle with employee morale, cash flow, or team management. It will be extremely difficult to overcome those roadblocks unless you're authentic and realize that your situation will likely be resolved much sooner and more efficiently if you seek support from your peers or a coach.

You don't have to take to Facebook and announce your problems to the world. Instead, you can get a coach, mentor, or confidant and discuss it with them in private. The best approach is to find a coach who has experience in your industry or with whatever personal challenges you are facing. They are much more relatable. You can also peruse books, or podcasts, with positive messages (like this one) or take any number of routes to reach out to those around you. Don't be afraid to leverage your network and seek advice from people familiar with your situation.

Consider the weight-loss example once again: yes, it's wonderful to work with a trainer to obtain support and guidance along your journey. Wouldn't it be better, though, to talk to someone who actually went through the weight-loss process and succeeded? All support is not equal. You must consider securing the right support to glean the best results. For example, even though my father was an entrepreneur as am I, he didn't provide the most relevant advice when I had business problems to discuss. Why? He didn't understand my business, and his experience was completely different. I could speak to him about macro entrepreneurial challenges but not micro ones. Instead, I approached a fellow entrepreneur in the same industry when discussing specific scenarios, and we were able to bounce ideas off each other and come up with the best solution.

BUT WHAT ABOUT FEAR?

In order to correct a problem or mend a mistake using the habit of habit-making, you need to be true to yourself. Continuing to run away from your fears or turn a blind eye to adversity will lead to a lack of confidence and likely backfire. I've found it is a better option to turn and willingly face challenges with openness, even though this can be completely scary and sometimes even overwhelming.

Public speaking, for example, is a big fear for many people, and many avoid it altogether. If you are an entrepreneur or leader, though, you will most likely have to address public speaking at some point in time, even if it's as little as holding an office or family meeting that requires you to offer inspiring words to the team. Being fully authentic means admitting this shortcoming, and being visionary means committing to changing it for the better.

Different people have different strengths. If you're a computer-science genius who has created a stellar new company, yet you're introverted, you will want to ensure that you have someone who is strong at building relationships with customers and can close deals for you. There is a good chance the business will not succeed the way you want it to unless either you learn to face your fears and learn how to leverage and sell, or you find someone in or out of your network who can. When authenticity is a core value, such an honest assessment is commonplace.

Before I sold my business—more on that in a minute—I discovered I hadn't put too much consistent effort into defining what the core values of the business were, so I decided to invite my staff to contribute ideas. I suggested everyone write down what the company meant to them in one core value, and I condensed the responses into a set of core values. We discussed them in all monthly meetings and looked for examples of how we were applying these core values in the business. The entire process forced me to look my own shortcomings in the face and have the tough discussions we weren't having before.

LESSONS LEARNED

After realizing a huge disconnect with my employees, I looked into ways to boost morale and reengage them. Prior to selling the business, I had a split team with a small staff locally in Utah and a large team in India. In the past, I was leery of forming personal relationships with my team—to the point that employees just thought I didn't like them because I wasn't fully engaged, when this was far from true. They wanted more connection with me, but I would come in and just bust my ass all day. Any side chatter for me revolved around getting more business. My team, however, wanted to build a relationship with the boss. I now realize that I had been dropping the ball in the authenticity department and, in doing so, driving a wedge that made me appear less approachable. Before I left, I made a point to take time to break free, have a little down time, and talk about our weekends, families, activities, etc. It became another positive habit.

Connection and being genuine are critical in the quest to form long-lasting, positive habits, but it's not always easy to go it alone. My staff needed a push in their work. A basketball player needs a boost from their coach. A struggling family member needs your positivity to get back on track. We all need support and leadership, and it starts with being authentic, expressing it by being true to yourself, taking consistent action, and leveraging help from others. In time, people will come to you for your inspiration, habits, and strength. By loosening your grip on who you're pretending to be or dropping your guard just a little, you might find *that thing*—whatever it is—that has been eluding you for so long. Maybe it's fulfillment, happiness, or peace.

CHAPTER NINE

———

BEHIND THE SCENES

SETTLING THE LAWSUIT AND SELLING THE BUSINESS

The lawsuit with my ex-business partner was a cluster. The original suit started because I felt she violated her noncompete by interfering in the business. At the time, I owed her $350,000 from the buyout to be paid in four payments over a two-year period. After an internal investigation, I held back the first payment and sent her notice. She then sued me. Once I was served those papers, I fell into a rage. I called my lawyers and my father for advice, and I countersued her for breach of contract and a litany of other things. The battle had begun.

Her sister and brother-in-law were still working for me in Idaho, but I never spoke to them about it—or anyone in my company. One year into the lawsuit with her, they resigned within a week of each other, and I found out they started a new business with her. They both had signed noncompetes with me, which I felt they violated by this action. This enraged me and pissed me off to no end. I reacted the only way I knew at the time: emotionally. I sued them both and the new company my ex-business partner started that hired them. Now there were four lawsuits going on.

I hid the struggle from everybody, taking on a lot emotionally and financially. I was trying to run the business and keep employees motivated, clients engaged, bills paid, lawyers on point, and so on, and I kept it all to myself. Why? Although I'd made progress with my employees relationship-wise, I didn't want to distract anyone from their work, and I didn't want them to think they were on a ship that was going down. I wanted them to be as focused as possible. This level of stress completely elevated all the bad habits in my life. To escape from it, on weekends I would go out to drink, smoke, self-medicate, and isolate myself. I fell into those same patterns: I wasn't working out and was depressed, constantly feeling sorry for myself. I felt trapped.

To complicate the situation further, I decided to expand

back into New York after the purchase. The company took out a half-million-dollar line of credit with Chase Bank, which I had to personally guarantee to help with the expansion and the legal fees. When the company was $280,000 into that line, we had our worst-performing year and actually lost money, as previously mentioned. The bank reviews company's finances yearly, and that year, we had lost money. So, without warning, the bank turned that $280,000 into a seven-year, high-interest loan and cut off the money line. My financial stress skyrocketed.

This period also brought about multiple depositions, both of which I flew to Idaho to take and which I had to pay my lawyer to fly to give. I had four depositions over the course of two years. A trial has many rules, but in a deposition, attorneys can ask any question. They're both difficult, but depositions, in particular, are highly stress-inducing for that reason.

During the third year of the four-suit fight, we got a notice the judge had retired. The case needed to be reassigned, which took another six months to get it back on the docket. Why? Maybe nobody wanted to take it. I wouldn't have blamed them.

AN ALMOST SETTLEMENT

Over the course of the six-year period, both sides filed

hundreds of motions back and forth. This is not an exaggeration! These motions had anything to do with throwing out evidence, filing additional complaints, sharing confidential information, and so on—all on top of the original complaints. During this time, I was borrowing money on the credit line to pay bills, paying back a $500,000 loan I had taken to buy the company, and still covering payroll expenses for seventy-five employees.

It felt a lot like my gambling days, when I was just shifting money around from one place or another, and this included my personal account, which I dipped into often to cover payroll.

While this was going on, my ex-partner was still reaching out to people at my company, which enraged me even more. When I found this out, I'd report it back to my lawyer. It went on and on and on, and to say it was bitter would be the understatement of the year. I was fueled with rage. I felt like she was screwing me while, at the same time, production in my international office was plummeting—a fact I attributed to her having an affair with one of my directors in the India office.

It was all too much. I had an opportunity to settle for far less than what I would eventually settle for. We were negotiating back and forth, and a number was put forward. I agreed to this, only for my ex-business partner's attorney to come back and ask for slightly more. This enraged me, and that old mentality of me getting screwed came back, creeping into my head. As much progress as I had made and as much as I had learned, when it came down to it, I said, "No, let's go to trial." I figured the trial would cost just as much, and I wasn't going to lose in these negotiations. It actually hurts to recount this, not because it would ultimately cost me several hundred thousand dollars more, but because, looking back, I realized I had not truly evolved from my old self. Those old mentalities overtook the new thought process I had been living by.

Why? I allowed my ego to get in the way because I thought she was bettering me in the negotiation. Instead of focusing on what the better outcome would be for me to move on with my life, I just had to win. Since I didn't feel like I *was* winning, I said, "Screw it, let's just go to trial." It came back to my gambling mind: I'd spent so much already, right? Might as well go to trial. If I lost, the worst thing would be that I'd just declare bankruptcy, so why not roll the dice?

That was a big mistake and another huge step in my evolution of understanding that even though I said I wanted to change, even though I was doing certain things to change, I wasn't ready. I wasn't thinking that even if I won, she could appeal—a move that would cost another year or two of my life. That decision kept me stuck in the same place—a place I was telling everyone who would listen that I wanted to get out of. As hard as it is to admit the truth, when it came down to it, I could not get out of my own way.

ANOTHER BATTLE

Throughout these later stages of the process, I not only battled with my ex-partner, but I also battled with my lawyers, especially with the lead attorney. I felt like they would only do things a certain way and were charging me for unnecessary services, like a jury consultant and an expert witness for the trial—both of which I was adamantly against, said I couldn't afford, but somehow got anyway. He kept telling me I wasn't allowing him to do his job and was insistent. Meanwhile, my fees continued to skyrocket as I implored him to keep costs down. We threatened to fire each other multiple times.

At one point, I had my father get on the phone with him because I could not speak to him, and this was just a couple of weeks before the trial. He had no flexibility whatsoever, so he hired a jury consultant anyway. The consultant told me how I should answer questions on the stand, what to wear, and so forth—all things that were completely against what I was going through at the time, which was being authentic and leading that activated life. My attitude was positive at this point, but I was being held back. I remember testifying on the stand during the trial and curbing my answers because I had the jury consultant in the back of my head telling me things. I didn't feel comfortable on the stand, and I didn't feel like myself. We would review testimony every day at lunch—me and five attorneys (of which I only wanted two). It was mentally exhausting.

Because I was a more authentic person and speaking my story to people, discussing the mistakes I'd made, and being more engaged with my employees, I decided I was going to do Facebook Live throughout my trial to keep everyone updated. The last thought entering my mind was that it might be used against me, but that's exactly what opposing counsel tried to do. When I was on the stand, they tried to entrap me into perjuring myself, asking questions about topics I'd discussed in my video. I was scared shitless. *Did I perjure myself?* I wondered. I really didn't know. This was the second day of the trial, and I was so drained. The judge ultimately dismissed the jury, listened to the video, and eventually said that it wasn't evidence. The opposing counsel couldn't submit it.

In the following days, we called to the stand the company's original attorneys who negotiated the original purchase agreement between myself and my former partner. The current attorneys told me they would be allowed to testify, so we spent days with them preparing. But, when it came down to it, the judge wouldn't allow it. This was a real blow, because they knew intimate details of the violations I believed my ex-business partner committed. The ironic thing is I questioned my attorney multiple times about whether or not they'd ever be allowed to testify. If they weren't, I didn't want to spend weeks interviewing them and prepping, get charged for all of it, and then not be able to use them. They insisted they would be able to testify, and then they weren't!

On the opposing side, they called all the former employees in India they could find and presented emails in which I was expressing frustration almost on a daily basis with my India office. This stemmed from them not being able to keep the infrastructure up. The computers and phone lines were not working for multiple days over several weeks, and no one over there was trying to solve the problem. There were many damning emails because I was very annoyed that we couldn't get our infrastructure all of a sudden. I was convinced that my ex-partner was over there having a relationship and sabotaging the office, hurting sales. Basically, the opposing side didn't have evidence to show they were right, but they had evidence to show I was a jerk. And it was true. The emails showed I was a jerk. It was a personal attack on me and my credibility. When you bias a jury, it's easy to get one or two people not to like you. Then the facts don't matter. However, the fact that I was a jerk and not a good leader at the time? Well, those facts are 100 percent true.

JUDGMENT—SORT OF

After six days of trial, five days on the stand, and twenty-something combined witnesses, the jury went back for deliberation. They were out for six hours. When they returned, they ruled I owed my ex-partner the $350,000— the amount we started arguing about in the first place. They also ruled in my favor, saying damages to me amounted to $260,000. In my mind, I thought, *Okay, so I owe her $90,000.*

Not so fast.

The judge ruled that because she was the prevailing party, I had to cover her attorney's fees for the judgments over which she prevailed. He said he wouldn't certify the ruling until we agreed on those fees. This was in August 2017.

I thought it was all going to end soon. Then I discovered they had thirty days to file their interpretation of the fees. Then we had between thirty and sixty days to respond. Then the judge had more time to review. Then she was threatening to appeal the decision. This song and dance went on for ten months, all while my attorney fees continued to rack up.

SETTLING—AND SELLING

As the lawsuit floundered on, I also realized I wanted out of my company. I was in a good place personally, and I wasn't running the business to the extent that I used to run it. I was no longer passionate about the staffing industry. I was at a positive point: I had hired a coach, was being more optimistic, and was active in YEC and Unconventional Life. I had a better attitude and was clearer about what mattered to me.

In short, I was no longer fulfilled with finding clients candidates but was more fulfilled mentoring others, working with nonprofits, building stronger relationships within my tribes, doing epic things like climbing Kilimanjaro with LLS, and so forth.

Still, I knew I couldn't sell the business with a lawsuit hanging over me. This was on my mind 24-7, preventing my ability to have any kind of personal relationship with anybody. Well into 2018, the motions kept firing back and forth. Around that time, I also started shopping the company and knew four or five potential buyers who might be interested. Ultimately, it came down to two companies: one of them happened to be my best friend—the one who I almost went into business with in New York all those years ago.

Unbeknownst to me, he called my ex-business partner up, whom he knew from the time we both worked together in New York years prior, and without asking me, helped negotiate a settlement: I'd give her the $350,000 and we'd be done—ironically, the same amount she initially sued me for six damn years before. She agreed. My lawyers were furious, and for a second, so was I. My first thought was, *How dare you go behind my back and call her?* I never said that to him, though, and it went away very quickly. In the past, I would've held on to it. It was a sign I was really ready to drop my ego and settle. My lawyers were adamantly against the decision, but I went forward. I knew the only way to settle the case was for me to sell the company. I warned him not to buy the business because I wasn't that optimistic about it, as I'd scaled down a lot. Still, he wanted to add tech to his portfolio, so we ended up negotiating a deal, and he purchased the business. The irony of it all is sometimes hard for me to even believe, but this was flow working its magic.

So, in back-to-back weeks, I was able to settle the lawsuit and sell the company. I didn't make a killing on the sale at all. I used the money from the sale to settle the lawsuit and pay the mounting legal bills. All in all, I spent over $1 million on this lawsuit.

Today, I'm still working to pay some of these bills off, but it's over. I have my life back in my control, and no amount of money could ever change that. For the first time in ten years, after the suit, I felt a feeling of lightness. It didn't matter that I didn't know where my next paycheck was coming from. It didn't matter that I spent all this money on the lawsuit. It didn't matter that I didn't have much to my name at that time. It's all over, and that is priceless!

LESSONS LEARNED

The lawsuit was one of the biggest mistakes of my life, and I was worried that I would lose it all. I played out the worst-case scenario in my mind, and I acted as if it had already happened! I call this the "What If" syndrome. How many of us do this? And why? It is such a waste of energy because 99 percent of the time, the things we worry about never occur. Nonetheless, my mindset wasn't at this place at the time, and doomsday was all I thought about. So I prepared as if I was going to go bankrupt.

I took out a home equity line against my house so I could generate another $100,000 and suck the equity out so my house could not be taken from me. I put that money into the bank and began taking withdrawals. Over the next ten weeks, I'd withdraw it in $9,999 intervals—just under the government cash reporting limit—and hide it in safes and banks protected by Indian laws that did not have to report to the government. These places exist in the US, and I researched and found them! I found a bank in California that was protected by these very laws, so I traveled there, taking two trips with $50,000 in my carry-on. I also took withdrawals from credit cards, stashing cash in a safe in the house. All along, I was preparing that I would lose the case, declare bankruptcy, and at least have this money I was stashing away to live on.

Looking back, this behavior was manic and mad. I was delusional and caught in my own thoughts and my own story. I kept repeating it over and over, and I convinced myself it was truth.

Well, the bankruptcy never happened, but that obsessive, negative behavior pattern reared its ugly head. I was nervous and freaking out. Even if I had to lose everything, I was bound and determined to win a little.

During the suit itself, when I had an opportunity to get out and settle, I didn't. I chose more chaos and turmoil, and I continued my pattern of erratic decisions and behavior. I was convinced I was a changed person, but I wasn't. I needed to go through one more huge lesson to put my ego in check once and for all. It goes to show that we are always a work in progress, and all we can do is tackle each day and each challenge head-on, be authentic, and learn from past mistakes.

CONCLUSION

THE FUTURE

The lawsuit was the worst business decision I ever made, and look at the mess it caused. The only thing I can do now is accept the consequences, learn from them, and teach others so they don't make the same mistakes I did. I want readers to understand that there is another way to approach high stress situations and that my decisions are an example of why emotional decision-making is the worst decision-making. The aftermath has major ramifications on all areas of our lives.

I know bitching and moaning won't change anything. It will only leave me in a negative state of mind and with a heavy feeling. This new perspective has allowed me to understand and manage stressful situations in a positive way. I know there is a reason I am going through this, and I understand there are lessons to be learned and shared with others. I know it's okay to be angry. We are human after all. However, anger can be a fleeting feeling that can be released instead of one that festers. Life isn't scripted. There will be more challenges to come and more people who might betray or disappoint me. I now understand it is the way I will handle those situations that will make me who I am. The key is to stay authentic and to learn and grow from those experiences.

I found many takeaways in the book *The Obstacle Is the Way* by Ryan Holiday, a fascinating look at self-belief and confidence. If you are dropped in a maze, for example, there are walls and dead ends blocking you from finding the way out. Most people will look for ways around, over, under, or through. No exit strategy will be successful, though, if you don't have the belief you'll make it. The maze is an obstacle you want to conquer, similar to the many obstacles we face in life. The only way through is to meet the obstacle head-on. The maze in this case becomes a conduit to self-confidence.

For me, the lawsuit was a major obstacle, and I met it head-on. That is the only way. As the title of Ryan's book states, the obstacle is the way. I couldn't avoid it, be angry with it, or suppress it. I couldn't smoke it away or gamble it away. Too many fallbacks allow us to avoid obstacles instead of using them to pave the road to the lives we want to lead. The path forward is directly through the challenges you are trying to overcome.

HOW TO ACTIVATE AND OVERCOME

Despite years of betrayal, adversity, and uncertainty, I am motivated now to give back, to pay it forward. I've finally settled the lawsuit and sold my business. Yes, I have legal bills, and sometimes the financial side of things can be extremely depressing if I let it be. I realize for the first time in my life, though, that *it's only money*. Whatever happens, I will deal with it in a much healthier way than I ever would have been able to before without the tools I now have.

Coming to grips with the fact that I control my state of mind—not circumstances that surround me—helped to bring out what was important to me. It's not how much money I can make or how big a company I can build. Instead, life is about giving back, helping others become the best they can be, and making a difference. I wrote this book because I don't want others to make the same mistakes I did, or at the least, I'd like to be able to share a different way to think about how you handle the challenges in your life. I may not know the right way to approach different situations, but I certainly know the wrong way to do it. That knowledge is enlightenment in itself, and it has helped me evolve into the person I am.

Remember, once you fire a bullet, you can't take it back, so fire wisely. I never knew six years ago that I'd be embroiled in a heated lawsuit tying up close to a million dollars and a good chunk of my life. Knowing what I know now, I would not have handled the situation the same, but it did help me create positive habits. I hope you take away this key from this book: remember, you are in control of your decisions and the people you surround yourself with. Having the right support system is critical. For example, if you're having legal battles, your support network cannot be your family, lawyers, business partners, or friends. They all have biased opinions because of your relationship with them. Instead, tap into another entrepreneur, a coach, or a mentor who has had relatable experiences in their life. If you're struggling with your business, consider reaching out to someone who has been in the same situation before, someone in the same or a similar industry to yours who can offer relevant feedback.

PAYING IT FORWARD

Giving back is my key to escape the fray. It is important for me to be able to positively impact people. It fulfills a part of my mind, body, and soul that cannot be replicated by anything else I do. At least once a month, I volunteer to feed the homeless, sponsor charity events, fundraise, and participate in friends' charitable efforts.

Acting as a mentor for others is another way I give back. It's more of a consultative approach, whereby discussing *my* mistakes and why I made them provides a new framework on how they can work through their options. This book follows that vein. If you can take one idea from these pages and it helps you transform your thought process, improve your mindset, or find a life of fulfillment, I consider that a great success.

ACTIVATING A MOVEMENT

In late 2016, after I returned from my life-changing retreat in Bali with loads of momentum, I was scheduled to attend a yearly entrepreneurial retreat at Powder Mountain in Utah through the organization Young Entrepreneurial Council (YEC), a group I have been part of for years. I rode to the event with a good friend of mine, Parveen Panwar. On the trip, he looked over at me and said something I'll never forget, "I'm going to activate everybody at this event."

"What? You're going to do what?" I replied. I had no idea what he was talking about. "What do you mean, you're going to activate everyone?"

"I'm just going to make sure that everybody has really high, positive energy, regardless of what is going on with their work or their personal life," he replied. "I'm going to make sure they're having a great time, they're focused, and they're full of passion about everything we're doing this weekend."

His spirit for this idea was infectious. I still didn't really know what the hell he was talking about, but in the spirit of competition, I said, "You know what? I'm going to activate more people than you." It started as a joke, but that weekend, we began talking to people and getting them pumped up about life. As the energy level in the room steadily rose, we knew we were on to something.

After the event, a few of us decided to continue the idea of activation further. We planned to create a website, but before we even got started, a couple of people from the event contacted us with an idea to make Activation T-shirts. We had a group of about a dozen Activated entrepreneurs who were really behind the message, and we thought we'd wear the shirts to the South by Southwest Festival in Austin, Texas, that following month to surprise Parveen, the one who had come up with the idea. He'd traveled home and was not privy to the T-shirt goings-on.

Instead, we switched up the plan and proposed we each create our own Facebook video, explaining what Activation meant to us to surprise him. Slowly, about ten or so videos started trickling in, and they were getting amazing engagement. Over the next couple of weeks, over one hundred entrepreneurs in our network and beyond reached out, asking how they could get involved and support the Activation movement. Bingo. From this, we put together a website (imactivated.com) and developed a set of core values outlined by the acronym PAPER.

POSITIVITY, AUTHENTICITY, PASSION, EMPATHY, RESILIENCY

Positivity is simple but carries enormous impact. Smiling at a stranger, for example, sounds like a small thing, but it can change someone's day, or at least brighten that particular moment. I mentioned before that I used to walk down the streets of New York and, when someone was looking at me, think, *What the F are you looking at?* Taking the exact opposite approach and smiling at that person—and maybe even saying hello—is such a lighter feeling to carry around...proof a small change can make a big difference.

Authenticity is a big one for me. It doesn't make a difference what your boss, mother-in-law, or coworker thinks about you, as examples. Be authentic to who you are. There will be people in your life who like you and people who don't. It's not something you can control, so it's not something you should worry about. You can, however, control being true to who you are and what you represent.

Passion is another way of saying hustle at whatever you're doing. Don't do anything half-assed. Remember, it's either a "Hell yes" or "Hell no."

Empathy pays it forward, and I'm a big believer that if you pay it forward, it will always pay you back. I live this through the philanthropy I participate in. Incorporating volunteer work into your schedule once a month can have a tremendous positive impact.

Resiliency is your key to endurance. We all will get knocked down in life, but it doesn't matter how many times you get knocked down or how many times you fail. Instead, what matters is that you get back up, dust yourself off, and take control of your own fate by paving your path forward. Nobody—not the government, ex-business partners, your family, or your friends—can stop you from designing the future you want, no matter how many failures you overcome along the way.

One of the positives we hope to accomplish with Activation is to see people take action. The world is full of so much negativity these days, and it's easy to get wrapped up in it to a point of inaction. Sitting at a computer writing comments on Facebook is basically a waste of time if you don't follow it up with any action. Getting out there and actually having an impact by getting your hands dirty to fix what you perceive to be a problem is where everyone can be impactful.

Our goal at Activation is to inspire and support the community we are building.

F.A.T.E. SERIES

As I worked on writing this book and lost interest and passion in running my business, I found another passion: writing the F.A.T.E. series published on Arianna Huffington's platform Thrive Global and on the platform Medium. F.A.T.E.—From Addict to Entrepreneur—details former addicts in the depths of their darkest days. In my interviews with those profiled, I discuss those dark days, how they overcame them, the traits that addicts and entrepreneurs share, the companies they have built, and how they are giving back to society. I'm even looking to turn this into a TV show. The F.A.T.E. series is extremely rewarding to me, and I have built a F.A.T.E. platform to work with entrepreneurs dealing with addiction or addictive behaviors. More information on this can be found at http://michaelgdash.com/fatemasterclass. It's a complete 180 from being in the corporate staffing world: now, I've written a book, started speaking publicly about my journey, and lead the F.A.T.E. series so others know there's another way to approach things. They know they're not alone. They don't have to isolate themselves. For me, having the right mentor/teacher/coach is extremely important when it comes to overcoming adversity. My goal in life now is to be that for others to show they can overcome whatever adversity they're facing.

LESSONS LEARNED

Chasing a high was all I knew for a long time in my life. That's who I was, and it sucked the life out of me. Now, I know life isn't about chasing money or searching for any other short-term fix; instead, it's about experiencing growth, incorporating lessons learned, loving myself, and passing it on to others.

I struggled recently when I got a look at my lawyer bill. I

knew it would be high, but it was much higher than even I had anticipated. It shocked me and, for the day I received it, knocked me off target. In the old days, I'd just smoke the problem away. If I steered into a rut, I got lazy. I let things distract me and lost discipline. Thanks to my new-found clarity, I can pull myself out of ruts like this a lot quicker now. I'm resilient. I've been knocked down time and again, and I will continue to get back up. Instead of focusing on money, I'm focusing on being fulfilled in a different way, being a positive influence, and giving back.

We forget how privileged we all are, and we take many things for granted. Most people tend to complain when things don't go their way. Instead of listening to the voices in our heads, we should use our true voices that are connected to our souls to be authentic to who we are and take action that makes a difference. We can all do our part. We can treat the person next to us a little nicer, smile at a stranger, or hold the door open for someone. It's the little things done by big-hearted people that bring light to someone's day and then, in return, impact you.

It can be hard to bring light to others if you can't see it yourself. Many people let the challenges of life beat them down and get the better of them. It's very important to have fun and joy in life, especially when the going gets tough. How can you do it? Go ahead, schedule fun! Make a habit of it.

I started scheduling fun after Bali, and it works well. I did simple things like organizing a Dirty Dash 5K mud run through an obstacle course. I gathered ten people together, some I knew and others who were friends of friends, we suited up in our Activation T-shirts, and we had a muddy blast. I booked a sushi-making class for ten other friends even though I had no one committed at the time. I knew, living in flow, it would come together, and it did. These are two simple examples. Why? I ask, why not? Experiences are far more important to me than money or possessions. They're chances to bring friends or family together, build deeper connections, and have a positive, fun time that can help balance out the adversity that may be going on in our lives.

As an influencer, I have focused my mission on bringing positivity and inspiration to others and making a lasting impact. I am doing this through speaking engagements, consultations, and future masterminds. You can find more information at my website: michaelgdash.com. Working with others to align them with their goals and hold them accountable to being the best they can be will allow them to share their unique gifts with the world. If you're a leader—of a company, of a team, of a family, of a household—you are an influencer, too, and you have the capacity to change people who look up to you. You can change their mindset, show them a different way, and get them involved. When you find positivity and transform your life by being authentic in your beliefs and actions, you have the ability to inspire others to do the same.

It all starts with you.

ABOUT THE AUTHOR

MICHAEL G. DASH is an entrepreneur, author, recovering addict, speaker, philanthropist, and thrill seeker. He founded the F.A.T.E. series (From Addict to Entrepreneur) published on Thrive Global and Medium, and rolled out a F.A.T.E. program to help entrepreneurs dealing with addiction, which he looks forward to growing. Information can be found at http://michaelgdash.com/fatemasterclass. He is the co-founder of imactivated.com, a social movement focused on inspiring a culture of positivity, authenticity, passion, empathy, and resilience. Michael is an avid volunteer, fundraiser, and mentor, and is dedicated to bringing positive change to leaders of all kind. You can reach out to him regarding partnering or other opportunities at michaelgdash.com.